Every Child Deserves A Champion

Including the Child Within You!

Every Child Deserves A Champion

Including the Child Within You!

Bob Danzig

With Callie Rucker Oettinger

Child & Family Press
Washington, DC

Child & Family Press is an imprint of the Child Welfare League of America. The Child Welfare League of America is the nation's oldest and largest membership-based child welfare organization. We are committed to engaging people everywhere in promoting the well-being of children, youth, and their families, and protecting every child from harm.

CHILD WELFARE LEAGUE OF AMERICA, INC.
HEADQUARTERS: 440 First Street, NW, Third Floor, Washington, DC 20001-2085
E-mail: books@cwla.org
Website: www.cwla.org

CURRENT PRINTING
10 9 8 7 6 5 4 3 2 1

Book cover and book design by Tammy S. Grimes
www.tsgcrescent.com • tsgcrescent@charter.net

Printed in the United States of America

ISBN # 0-87868-885-4

Library of Congress Cataloging-in-Publication Data
Danzig, Robert J., 1932-
  Every child deserves a champion : including the child within you! /
Bob Danzig, with Callie Rucker Oettinger.
      p. cm.
Originally published: South Orange, NJ : Professional Bi-Cultural Develpment, 2002.
  ISBN 0-87868-885-4 (alk. paper)
  1. Encouragement. 2. Self-confidence. 3. Achievement motivation in children. 4. Mentoring.
5. Heroes. 6. Kindness. I. Oettinger, Callie Rucker. II. Title.
  BF637.E53D36 2003
  177'.7--dc22
                                                        2003018507

Dedication

With ongoing respect and admiration for PBD's gift

of treasuring each of our five children

and

being such a perfectly unique champion framing our beloved

Mary Beth, Marsha, Darcy, Steven, and Matthew.

Acknowledgments

Each book is merely a bubble of an idea at conception. Shape, dimension, scope, and purpose flow from all those talents that join in "birthing" that book. *Every Child Deserves a Champion: Including the Child Within You!* has enjoyed a flowing river of gifted participation from all those whose stories underscore the champions who guided them. This bubble—now book—is also manifest with the crisp creative mind and imagination of Robin Sidel, whose touching stories punctuate as Spiritual Oasis highlights. As always, all of the above has been beautifully shaped by the magical embroidery of the very large talents of Callie Rucker Oettinger. And, a deep bow to Tammy Grimes who shared the soul of her creative gifts in designing this work, so that it is eye-candy for the reader. Each and all have abundant gratitude from this author whose idea "bubble" might well have remained just that. The talent of all provide the privilege of a book now born. Thank you all.

—BOB DANZIG

TABLE OF CONTENTS

Chapter 1

CHAMPIONS

Spiritual Oasis

Chapter 2

FROM THE CHAMPIONS OF FRIENDS & FAMILY

Spiritual Oasis

Chapter 3

A WHOLE NEW WORLD OF CHAMPIONS

Chapter 4
OUTLETS TO DISCOVER OUR CHAMPIONS

Spiritual Oasis

oreword

As I sat there in the Drewry Room of the College of Journalism, at the University of Georgia, I clung to every word Bob Danzig said as if he were only speaking to me and not the other fifty or so people in the room. Captivating. That is the only word I can think of to describe him that day. This man was telling my story—only, it was his own. He had come from the same less-than-perfect background that I had. Yet, there he was, the vice president of a world-renowned publishing company telling me that I could do the same thing. "You are talented," he said. Me? Talented? Sure, I know how to survive and how to work hard to get everything I want, but I never considered that talent. Bob made it sound believable, and I was sold. The more I listened to him, the more I wanted to hear. I wanted him to keep telling me how far in my life I could go. There was a reason he was so enthralling, but I did not realize it until later. Immediately after his speech, I went up to him and he grabbed me—I mean he physically put his arm around me and pulled me close to him. And it wasn't just with me; he was like that with everyone who came up to talk to him. Normally I would have felt threatened, but with him, I was totally comfortable, as if I'd known him for a long time.

"What do you want your life to be?" he asked. Stunned, I stammered, "I want to be a journalist." At the time I thought I could have come up with something better to say. Without missing a beat, Bob said, "You can do it, you will do it, because you are who you are and you are wonderful." That just made my day. I walked away from that room floating on his words and repeating them over and over in my head. Graduation was fast approaching and I was feeling less than confident about my chances of getting a job right out of college. Bob's words took away my worries.

I know people who think the power of positive affirmation is imaginary, but I can argue that point all day. Thinking positively has taken me a long way and I thank Bob for becoming not only a friend that day, but a "thread in my personal tapestry," as he is fond of saying.

Soon after meeting Bob, I accepted a summer magazine internship in New York. I decided to take a chance and to write Bob, explaining who I was, how he had spiritually enlightened me, and that I'd like a chance to "do lunch" when I arrived in Manhattan. Honestly, I never expected him to respond. After all, being a high-powered executive with a budding motivational speaking career doesn't leave much time for mentoring, I thought. But to my delight, he called me and said he would love to meet with me. Even more surprising, the day after I arrived in New York, the internship coordinator handed me a message from him. He had tracked me down before I had had a chance to get in touch with him! Amazing.

A few weeks later, we met for lunch and he beamed when he saw me. I didn't think he would remember me, but he grabbed me again and hugged me like we were old friends. Over lunch, I did most of the talking. He wanted to know everything about me—my childhood, why I chose the University of Georgia, what I wanted out of my summer in New York, and so on.

Bob adopted me that summer. He said he wanted to be my mentor and that he was going to make sure I had the best time I could in the city. He made good on his promise and I saw the theater, the ballet, and many other things I'd never had the opportunity to experience. Having grown up on the streets of New Jersey, these kinds of luxuries offered a whole new world to me.

I grew up the product of a broken home. My father left when I was four years old. My mother fled her duties soon after and my brother and I became my grandmother's responsibility. When my grandmother was diagnosed with a brain tumor in 1989, we siblings became wards of the state of New Jersey. My brother and I were separated and moved from one foster home to the next. A wonderful family who told me I could be anything I wanted, despite my humble beginnings, eventually adopted me. I learned that hard work and focus were all I needed to succeed. I could have become another foster home statistic, but I didn't want that to be my future. I finished college and now have a job at a newspaper doing exactly what I want to do with my career. And, champions in my life like Bob have ensured that I stay on a path to a lifetime of success.

—**KELLI PARKER**

Introduction

Every child deserves a champion. As a child growing up in the foster care system, this concept never crossed my mind. Now, however, the value of this statement guides my every step. As an adult reflecting upon his childhood, I am extremely thankful that I have had the good fortune to have had champions in my life—individuals who not only acted as springboards to opportunity, but as my greatest supporters. I was a diamond in the rough to them—a child needing someone who could see the worth in his potential and someone who had the patience to help a child smooth his jagged edges and shine.

I like to believe that I would have been as fortunate and achieved all I have today—a wonderful wife, five marvelous children, and three grandchildren, as well as over forty years with the Hearst Corporation as vice president of the company and CEO of the Hearst Newspaper Group—on my own, but when it comes down to it, it was the applause of a few key individuals that made the difference. *Every Child Deserves a Champion: Including the Child Within You!* was born from this realization and took root in the following story, which two hiking friends shared from their lives:

Shelly and Scott were one of the couples on a guided hike I took in the mountains of Santa Fe and Taos, New Mexico. The eighteen of us who had signed on for the week of hiking were chatting amiably on the first day, describing our families, our work, our passions, and our hobbies. Heads down, always on alert for unfriendly tree roots or stones ready to impede the trail, the easy, relaxed conversation allowed us to migrate from hikers to pals—a nice journey…

Inspired by the majesty of New Mexico's abundant sunrises, sunsets, and pure earthy beauty, our group covered miles of trails through the beautiful state, as well as through our personal lives during a week when quiet was an everyday companion.

Mid-day became our time to sit, lunch, stretch, and grow in knowledge of each other. Eye-to-eye conversation was so much more compelling than the eye-to-back chats limited by our single-file hiking patterns.

"We've been blessed with our three treasured daughters and our marvelous son, Danny," said Scott as he described his children. His wife, Shelley, talked enthusiastically about each daughter and the unusual fact that all were married and lived within one block of each other—"Our own little compound," she asserted. "And," Shelley said, "the family has the further good news of the youngest child, Danny, living at home with us." Danny was a software engineer who had recently earned his master's degree in computer science. Their family profile resonated with me since my wife and I also have three daughters. And, the youngest of our two sons, Matt, was also a recent college graduate who was living at home with us until his horizon of work defined where he needed to relocate to.

On the final day of our hiking trip, Shelley, a university professor, shared a story over our mid-day lunch about the multi-university study team she was part of, which was examining the phenomenon of so many male children of famous athletes being born with autism and other serious emotional and physical challenges. She commented that the task force was attempting to identify common characteristics that these athletes might share. One early observation she said, was the enormous chasm between the public adoration these athletes had in their lives, and the fact that they returned home to a challenged child who was emotionally unaffected by their fame. The gap these athletes travel between devoted fans and the private anguish of the challenged child is an extraordinarily wide one.

As Shelley talked about the very real psychological difficulties such athletes face, her husband, Scott, leaned across the picnic table and said that his wife had earned the right to understand that difficulty, because they had had a personal experience in dealing with a challenged child. "You see," he explained, "our Danny was born with a mild cerebral palsy that left his right arm limp and unable to function. He also has a severe limp in his right leg. One day, when Danny was four years old, he was in the neighborhood with all his young friends playing made-up games. All the children had learned to tie their shoelaces about that time and a game of choice that day was to form a circle and compete to see who could tie their shoelaces the fastest. All the children were in that circle, including Danny, who, because he had no use of his right hand, could not tie his shoelaces at all."

Scott told us that when Danny came limping home with a mournful sob, so conscious of his failed arm and hand, he looked down at Danny and promised himself that his son was going to live a life seeing possibilities rather than limitations. As Scott listened in anguish to Danny's sobs, and as he hugged Danny tightly, he committed himself to being an instrument to encourage his son to see all the possibilities. With the impetus of that thought, Scott decided to teach himself to tie his own shoelaces, using only his left hand. It took him two months to master the technique. Scott then began teaching Danny, who, accustomed to using only his left hand with the dexterity such use provides, became swift at tying his shoelaces with his single left hand in just a week.

Armed with his new capability, Danny went out into the neighborhood where his friends were having another shoelace-tying contest. Danny came home beaming with a cheek-to-cheek smile because he had won the contest. He looked up at his proud father and said, "Daddy, you are my champion."

As Scott shared this powerful story over our final hiking picnic lunch, he looked at me and said, "Every child deserves a champion." I looked back to Scott and said, "That, my friend, is a book waiting to be shared."

My intention in sharing the rich treasures of the stories that follow is to encourage you to have cause to reflect on those champions in your own life—yesterday and today—taking special time to consider the spiritual oasis following each chapter. Because the response to some of the stories appearing in my previous book, *Angel Threads*, has remained so strong, I have reprinted a few special ones here to emphasize the importance of champions in our lives. And, just as the yang is connected to the yin, my additional hope is that you will have cause to embrace every opportunity to be a champion for those you are privileged to influence. Regardless of age, each of us always has some of the child within us.

—BOB DANZIG

Spiritual Oasis

You are Worthwhile

You Are Full of Promise

You Are Unique in the Universe

There is Only One You

Only You Can:

lick your lollipop (and chew to the soft middle)

have your essence

blow your kiss

＊

wink your eye

give your hug

share your voice

choose your silence

feel your joy

explore your future

make your choices

express your gratitude

remember your yesterday

enjoy your laugh

shed your tear

choose your attitude

experience your spirit

share your love

ease your disappointments

have your giggle

share your goodness

remember your past...

＊

treasure your future

experience your joy

choose your pals

You Deserve:

peace

harmony

serenity

noble purpose

two-way love

comfort

self-esteem

a sense of belonging

a sense of self-identity

a sense of worthiness

a sense of competence

a sense of confidence

appreciation

approval

destiny

trust

celebration

humor

tomorrow

today

this moment

this second

You are Unique in the Universe

There is Only One You!

CHAPTER ONE

Champions

WHAT IS A CHAMPION?

The ordinary man is involved in action, the hero acts.
An immense difference.
—HENRY MILLER

Superman or Captain Marvel. If someone had asked me what a champion is when I was a child, I probably would have answered by naming these two superheroes of the day—or, perhaps, someone along the lines of Babe Ruth, Lou Gehrig, or Joe Louis. It would not have occurred to me to name one of the individuals in my life. As I mentioned in the Introduction, I spent my childhood growing up in the foster care system. During this time, I didn't realize how the kindness of a few key people could parallel the life-saving feats superheroes regularly performed. However, as I grew older and began to reflect on the impact certain individuals had had on my life, I realized that instead of muscles of steel, they protected me with the strength of their kindness.

Mae Morse, the social worker assigned to my movement from my fourth foster home to my fifth, opened my life to possibility when, at the end of our first meeting, she leaned in close to me and said, "Never forget—YOU ARE WORTHWHILE!"

EVEN TODAY, I CAN HEAR HER QUIET WHISPER TRUMPETING, "NEVER FORGET—YOU ARE WORTHWHILE!"

During that full year when she regularly came to check out my status, she reinforced the strength of my self-esteem by continually saying those three kind words at the conclusion of each of our meetings. By gifting me an extra measure of herself, she became the earliest champion in my life. Instead of wowing me with the ability to leap tall buildings in a single bound or to throw no-hitters, she helped enhance my power of self-confidence. I am convinced that had it not been for the three magic words Mae Morse said to me at the end of each of our meetings, I would not have the privilege of living such a rewarding life. Even today, I can hear her quiet whisper trumpeting, "YOU ARE WORTHWHILE!"

RECOGNIZING CHAMPIONS— AND CHILDREN

It does no harm just once in a while to acknowledge that the whole country isn't in flames, that there are people in the country besides politicians, entertainers, and criminals.
—CHARLES KURALT

When I first began asking friends for their opinions about a book championing the rights of children, many thought it was a great idea, and threw out such names as Paul Newman and Audrey Hepburn, who are world-renowned for their work benefiting children. Few suggested that what they themselves were doing in their own lives might constitute the work of champions, or that the child my title alluded to was defined by anything other than one of a young age. But as I continued to share the original concept of my title and did more research, I found myself redefining "a child" as an attitude rather than one of young age. And, when I came across one of Bill Cosby's insightful quotes—"It is popular today to say that we have to find the child within us. For me, this would be a short search."—I knew that I was moving in the right direction, expanding *Every Child Deserves a Champion* to include adult children as well.

When we grow older, I think many of us have a tendency to drop "the child within" off at daycare because we have so many "adult" responsibilities to take care of; the child simply gets in the way. A few years back, there was a college valedictorian whose graduation speech was televised on the evening news. While on stage, he cut off his long ponytail and proclaimed that on that day he was going undercover. He was going to wear his hair short and his face clean-shaven, and don suits to infiltrate the adult world. When I think about this valedictorian now, I wonder how successful he was—if he was able to maintain the balance between becoming an adult and remaining a child.

As the survivor of a heart attack, I've found that it is very important to have a balance between the adult and the child side of myself—to remember to pick up that inner child and not to leave him at "daycare" for too long. Following my heart attack, the doctors told me that I had to take it easy. I could not return to work right away. Fortunately, while in the hospital I met Gene Wald, who had also suffered from a heart attack and who became my "recovery pal" when we were both released from the hospital. What Gene did for me then, I realize now, was to awaken my inner child. We made model airplanes, went on walks, and regained our strength together. It reminds me of the turnaround that the adult Peter Pan, played by Robin Williams, made in the movie *Hook*. He had become so wrapped up in his work that he had forgotten about the childhood basics such as being spontaneous without being self-conscious, or courageously tackling a challenge because it was new, and because he didn't know enough to be afraid.

In one particular scene, Grandma Wendy asks Peter, "What is so terribly important about your terribly important business?" and Peter's son answers, "Well, you see, when a big company is in trouble, Dad sails in, and if there is any resistance, he blows them out of the water." Grandma Wendy's response is, "So, Peter, you've become a pirate."

WHAT GENE DID FOR ME THEN, I REALIZE NOW, WAS TO AWAKEN MY INNER CHILD.

As an adult, Peter encompassed everything he despised as a child. He had become so bogged down by the adult in him that he had even forgotten how to fly—how to feel completely free of the adult constraints, while still dealing with the responsibilities the adult world placed on him. However, once he was given another chance to "be a child," his life completely changed. By awakening his child within, he overcame the fears he developed as an adult and regained the confidence of his youth. And, he was able to do all of this because he had the support of people who believed in him. Gene Wald was instrumental in my heart attack recovery because he reintroduced simple childhood joys such as building model airplanes. Like *Hook's* Peter Pan, I was reminded how "to fly" again.

In our own way we each have the ability to champion children of all ages. We simply have to see within ourselves the ability to be champions and be open to the challenges. Blind schoolteacher Rich Ruffalo is one such person who discovered his potential tied to a greater purpose once he examined what was within him.

A CLEAR VIEW

"HAVE YOU NOTICED THAT I HAVE NOT BEEN LOOKING AT YOU?" HE ASKED. DURING MY *first meeting with Rich Ruffalo, he surprised me by asking me this question. I had first heard Rich's name spoken by university professor Dr. Rob Gilbert. I had just addressed his graduate class in sports psychology when Dr. Gilbert told me that Rich Ruffalo had spoken to his class a month before, and that he believed Rich and I would enjoy knowing each other.*

After a few failed stabs at phone tag, I finally made contact with Rich and made a date to visit him. When I arrived at his home, I rang the doorbell with a sense of excitement. As the door opened, I extended my hand in greeting. Standing before me was this giant of a man, well over six-and-a-half-feet tall, who looked like part of the interior line of a pro football team. Rather than shake my hand, he said, "Come here. I want to hug you!" He literally picked me up and I hung from his embrace, legs dangling like a Raggedy Andy doll.

Once he set me down, Rich asked that I follow him to his porch where we would chat. He walked in front of me, settled into a chaise lounge, and suggested I sit in the lawn chair next to him. Just as I began more formally to introduce myself, his six-year-old daughter Sara came bouncing onto the porch. She settled into her father's lap and asked whether they could sing their special song before she said "night-night." Rich pulled her up close to his cheek and Sara turned her sweet face to me, the guest audience, and beamed her radiant smile. Rich's baritone joined with her lovely soprano and they sang aloud, We Have Come To Teach. Four verses. In perfect harmony. Sara, wearing her pastel yellow Winnie-the-Pooh nightgown and the contented look of a loved child, nestled right up to her daddy's cheek. With the song concluded, Sara kissed us both and toddled off to sleep.

"I am a teacher," Rich said to me. He explained that he taught biology in a local high school, and had been honored by the Disney Corporation as the nationwide *teacher of the year. The song, he said, was the theme music for the event, and Sara had loved it so much that it had become their personal tradition for their evening goodnights.*

Rich then leaned his face towards me and asked, "Have you noticed I have not been looking at you?" I replied that I did, but thought that I had not yet said anything to compel his interest.

He drew a deep breath and told me that he had not looked at me because he

could not see me. He was blind. His sight, he said, had left him four years after college. As his sight dimmed, he said, it was replaced with a deep bitterness. Why me? *That became the question that would not leave his mind.*

HE TOLD ME HE HAD NOT LOOKED AT ME BECAUSE HE COULD NOT SEE ME.

With his teaching career threatened, only the participation in athletic events for the blind gave him any sense of relief and wholeness. He did continue to teach with the aid of a sighted proctor. Because he needed to raise the funds to pay for his travel to the athletic competitions, he contacted local organizations to sponsor him, and then would repay them by speaking about his experiences to their employees. Quite unintentionally, he found himself in demand as a speaker for a growing number of local

groups. Audience members, moved by his comments, encouraged him to become a professional speaker, as did his caring wife Diane. Although he started quite tentatively, Rich soon found himself in high demand as a polished and highly impactful professional speaker.

The trigger event, he told me, was his realization that he had a gift to share. It occurred at a St. Louis track event when he felt a tug on his sleeve, accompanied by a woman's voice telling him she was there with thirty-one children from the St. Louis School for the Blind. They had come, she said, "to touch you today."

Rich said he knelt down and each child rubbed his muscular arm, shoulder, and neck. When he stood to throw the javelin, he could hear the children cheering. Their voices gave him momentum, and that day he threw the javelin farther than he ever had before. More important than the gold medal he won, he said, was the vision he saw as the javelin left his hand; he was blind because others needed him to inspire them to choose to see the light of possibility rather than the grim dim of despair. Rich sensed that he could be a champion for the light even though he himself was anchored in visual darkness.

BEING OPEN TO CHAMPIONS

*Every moment is a golden one for him who
has the vision to recognize it as such.*
—HENRY MILLER

As Rich Ruffalo came to find the light in his darkness, I have found a similar brightness in the lives of children who have had a history of darkness. Since 1998, I have been a sponsor of Awards for Youth in Foster Care, a writing competition for foster children in New York City. For one of the competitions, the participants were asked to write two essays. The first was to cover the topic "How I've helped others" and the second was "Advice I'd give myself." The submissions I received were nothing less than spectacular. The one sad theme that ran throughout them, however, dealt with being open to the kindness of others. It reminded me of an experience I had early on in life.

Just out of high school, with no family, no money, and no specific aspirations, my first full-time job was in the wholesale mattress department of Montgomery Ward as a "climber." That task involved climbing up the ladder bins, which held the mat-tresses segregated by alphabet and number. For example, C-7 would have a certain single bed piece, while the crosswalk ladder at the top would lead to a B-7, which might be a queen-size mattress. Simply scurrying about each shift up the ladder, over the crosswalk, and pushing mattress pieces called out by the floor foreman off the very high pile, which were to be caught in a soft trampo-line, was not challenging, but was tiring as the day went by. It was around 4:00 P.M. on a Friday afternoon when I heard C-7, rather than the desired B-7, and my mattress got lift-off from me. Rather than landing on the trampo-

T HE ONE SAD THEME THAT RAN THROUGHOUT THE ESSAYS DEALT WITH BEING OPEN TO THE KINDESS OF OTHERS.

line, it squashed the foreman straight on. His next two words were my first exposure to corporate consequence: GET OUT!

That night I went to a teenage dance and met a high school pal who asked what I was doing. "I was just fired from Montgomery Ward," I said, and then explained the story of C-7/B-7. He then told me he was the office boy in the circulation depart-ment at the Albany *Times Union* and was being promoted to clerk. If I came down on

Monday morning, he said, he might be able to have me interviewed. However, he felt that I looked very young and thought that it would be helpful if I wore a hat—specifically a fedora. The next day I went to the Snappy Men's Shop on Central Avenue in Albany and bought my very first hat.

On Monday morning, I was inside the circulation department, application in hand, behind nine other guys who were also applying for the office boy job, but who had read about it in the classifieds. There was no obvious urgency to that lowest job in the department, thus the office manager would only take the applications in between handling other chores. At least an hour and a half went by and there we stood, each individual interviewee slowly "peeling off" as he handed in his application. I was the last in line.

When it came my turn, the office manager, Margaret Mahoney, a tiny woman not even five feet tall who at first glance resembled a pit bull, looked at me before taking my simple application and said, "I want to ask you a question."

"Yes, ma'am," I replied.

After what seemed like another hour of staring at me she asked, "Why are you wearing that hat?"

I explained that my friend suggested I looked too young and should wear a hat.

"But," she admonished, "you have been *inside* this department for over an hour and are supposed to take your hat off when you are inside."

I then whisked the hat off and explained to her that I had never had a hat before and did not know what to do with it. Her stern stare turned to a warm smile. To this day, I am convinced she gave me the job because I did not know enough to take off my hat.

I had not worked for that diminutive giant four months when she sat me down one Saturday morning during my shift and told me, "You are full of promise"—words I had never had spoken to me before, but which provided the fuel to ignite an engine of higher purpose.

Indeed, as I went to college at night for six years, then off to Stanford University on a journalism fellowship, and then nineteen years after I walked in the door as the office boy, was named publisher of the Albany *Times Union*, I always heard the echo of Margaret Mahoney's encouraging words in my mind.

I ALWAYS HEARD THE ECHO OF HER ENCOURAGING WORDS IN MY MIND.

In fact, when I first walked through the doors of the Hearst Corporate headquarters building to become the steward of all Hearst newspapers nationwide, I could hear Margaret saying, "You are full of promise." The years have not dulled the early shining thread she brought to my tapestry. She was never the pit bull that my first impression saw her to be. In fact, my memory only sees the sweetness of her smile and the elfin smirk she exuded when a customer thanked her for her caring attention. Her smile, her smirk, and her caring way were, I now realize, echoes of a champion rooting for my personal possibilities. Every day her memory reminds me of the importance of being open to others—and not asking "What's in it for me? Why is this person being nice to me? What do they want?" In fact, as I read through the submissions for Awards for Youth in Foster Care, the writing competition I previously mentioned, I thought about her. She saw in me what many of the social workers, whose letters accompanied the submissions as recommendations, saw in the children they work with—a child rich in potential, despite a rough start in life. Because the submissions I received spoke so strongly to me, I have woven a few of them throughout *Every Child Deserves a Champion*. The following represent two of the topics the children/young adults were asked to write about—"How I've helped others" and "Advice I would have given myself."

THE LONG CONVERSATION WITH MY FORMER SELF

by Qwonjit Nelson

I SAT DOWN WITH MY FORMER SELF AND TALKED WITH HER OVER A CUP OF COFFEE AT the local Starbucks while waiting for my bus. She began to tell me how she couldn't stand school and the way people make fun of her and call her names because of her shabby appearance. I saw that she had a lot of issues.

"What's wrong?" I asked as I brought the mug to my lips.

"Well, everything," she said. "My mother doesn't love me and my boyfriend is cheating on me and I'm just a wreck and…"

"And what?"

A tear fell from her face to the floor. "I don't know if I want to live. Things are so overwhelming, you know? What would you know," she then snapped. "You're in college and you're in a good position."

"Well, look Qwonjit, you can't let life get to you. If you let people see the buttons that tick you off, and the ones that get you aggravated, they'll only push them even more. You have to look deep within yourself and try to do the best that you can for yourself. You can't put all of the world's problems on your shoulders. Being a teen is hard enough. Why add more pressure to it?"

As she wiped her eyes, I could see the failed attempts of suicide on her wrists. "What's this?" I asked, pointing to her wrists.

"Nothin. Look, I don't want to talk, okay?" she replied, her eyes deeper than any I've ever seen. She definitely had a lot of issues.

"Sure. Whatever. Go ahead and hide your feelings. You're only eating yourself up," I told her. "Look, being in foster care isn't the end of the world, you know. Just think of it as a temporary blemish. It'll go away some day. But, for now, you have to live with it and make the most of yourself. You can't let words get to you. And besides, who's going to look after your sisters if you succeed in your attempts?"

"Well, you have a point there," she admitted.

I smiled. "Yes, and besides, the world would miss a terrific writer."

She laughed and took a sip of her coffee.

"Qwonjit, what you have to do now is use the foster care system to your advantage. They have many programs available for you and a lot of people who are willing to listen. That's only if you talk and express yourself—and smile!"

As my bus approached I walked towards the door and handed her my card. "Keep in touch," I said.

"Okay! Thanks," she said as she looked down at the card. It read: "Ms. Qwonjit Nelson, the person you are inside."

Sunshine and a Rainbow

by Merli Desrosier

What does it really mean to help someone? The greatest help I've been was *to my deceased mother Rosemarie Desrosier. Before she died, I was mommy's little helper. I used to help her cook and clean, but that's not how I helped her. I helped her by being there when my father used to beat her up to the point of being unconscious. I would stick by her until she gained her strength back and together we would cry. Although she was the one hurting, I hurt more because as young as I was, I couldn't fight. I could only help the situation by helping her heal.*

The violence went on for nine years. It wasn't until her last year on this earth that I realized that I was the only help she had. While she was pregnant, she was often very sick and unable to stand. Her disease, Sickle Cell, caused her sickness. Because of that, I would always do things that she needed me to do. I would sit by her and talk to her about the name of the baby, and laugh at the funny jokes, and about my imma-ture ways. My mother and I would often go to the park, and I'd make her sit on the swing, and try to push her. She never got off the ground, but I was always successful in putting a great big smile on her face. Although there were a lot of rainy days in my mother's life, I brought her sunshine and a rainbow.

When my mother died, although I was in grief, I knew she was resting in peace because my father wouldn't be able to hurt her anymore. I helped my mother through all those hard times because that's all I knew. That's how she brought me up— to help others. I also did it because I loved her and she meant the world to me. From that whole experience I learned that you should always cherish and help your parents because you never know what will come tomorrow. Helping my mother also prepared me for the many years of growing up I had to do for not only myself, but also for my little sister Marie. If it weren't for all that experience with my mother, I would be a lot less responsible. Although she is gone, I feel to this day I'm helping her by being mother to my sister, for raising my sister to understand what my mother made me understand—that education is important—it'll be the difference between being in my mother's situation or having control of our lives now and in the future. I'm also still helping my mother by studying law so that problems like my mother faced won't occur anymore. I'm happy to say that as a result of this my mother would've been happy because she has helped me to become what I am today—a beautiful young lady—and the successful woman I'll be tomorrow.

Spiritual Oasis

HOW GREAT THOU ART

by Robin Sidel

ebbie Wright still vividly remembers that awful day a few years ago. Nothing was going well in the office, and as housing commissioner of New York City, her presence was required at a ribbon-cutting ceremony for a new senior citizen center in East Harlem. It was snowing. She didn't have boots or an umbrella and she got caught in the typical tangle of uptown traffic.

When the car finally arrived at the senior center, she opened the door and peered out. Almost on cue, the bells from the nearby church began pealing a rendition of "How Great Thou Art," a favorite hymn of Wright's paternal grandmother, who had died more than ten years earlier.

"I've had a couple of really bad days when that song just appears. It's like she's watching me," said Wright, who is now chief executive officer of Carver Bancorp, the parent company of the nation's largest African American-owned bank.

Indeed, Debbie's grandmother, Maggie Wright, spent much of her life watching over other people. As a minister's wife in the segregated rural town of Bennettsville, South Carolina, the Philadelphia native was the grand dame of her family and the community. She worked with

I'VE HAD A COUPLE OF REALLY BAD DAYS WHEN THAT SONG JUST APPEARS.

her husband to build a church in spite of the Depression, serving as its organist, running fundraisers, and establishing a local home for senior citizens. Along the way, she put her five children through college. Widowed at a young age, she watched her son, Debbie's father, take over the family church.

And when her own children were grown, Maggie turned to the children of other people, taking more than twenty foster kids into her home.

Along the way, she also helped care for her granddaughter, Debbie, a premature baby who grew into a sickly child with severe allergies and asthma that often kept her home from school. She determined that her young granddaughter should receive the same medical care as the local white children, and somehow established a friendship with a white physician who snuck Debbie in a back door of the local hospital so that she could receive crucial allergy shots.

IT WAS THE CLASSIC DEFINITION OF AN EXTENDED FAMILY.

As the eldest child of the local minister and a prominent family, the young Debbie was strong-willed, smart, and surrounded by love and attention.

"When you grow up in a church, you have a lot of mothers, sisters, brothers, and grandparents. It was the classic definition of an extended family and it was a wonderful way to grow up," she said.

But she was happiest in her grandmother's company, delighting in their trips to the local Winn-Dixie supermarket or dropping by Sears to pick up the latest catalog delivery.

"We formed a very close bond. It was said that we were soul mates," said Wright, who credits her grandmother with instilling her confidence, perseverance, and independence.

That bond remained fast when, at the age of twelve, Debbie left Bennettsville for Dallas, where her father had accepted a position as chaplain at a Baptist college.

"It was hard on both of us," Wright recalled.

So while other teenage girls would spend hours on the phone gossiping with friends, Wright would be sharing stories with her grandmother back in Bennettsville.

Those telephone calls continued when Debbie, voted "most likely to succeed" in high school, headed east to Harvard University in 1975. College was an invigorating and frightening place for the minister's daughter, whose parents shunned alcohol and were disciplinarians.

THERE WAS NOT A SINGLE TIGHT SPOT WHERE I DIDN'T CALL HER.

"There was not a single tight spot where I didn't call her. She could hear it in my voice on the other end of the phone. What I valued in those phone calls was that in seven minutes, she would zero in on the big picture. She was the Rock of Gibraltar for me."

And throughout it all, Maggie would be reminding her granddaughter to go to the music store and pick up some sheet music for "How Great Thou Art."

"She had about twenty versions. She was always looking for a certain type of arrangement," Wright recalled.

The phone calls have stopped now and Maggie's piano sits in Wright's New York City apartment. Wright was in graduate school when her grandmother passed away, but Maggie Wright has not left her granddaughter's side.

Indeed, Wright has often relied on her grandmother's memory over the years as she earned bachelor's, business, and law degrees from Harvard, bargained with Wall Street dealmakers as an investment banker, wrestled politicians, battled skeptics, and defended Carver against a hostile takeover.

WRIGHT OFTEN CONSIDERS HER GRANDMOTHER'S LIFE.

And the sound of her grandmother's laughter resounded in her mind in 1999 when people questioned the ability of Wright, who never before held a position in corporate America and had no experience in commercial banking, to lead the money-losing Harlem-based bank into a new era.

"She'd be so resolute about it. She would have been totally nonplussed," said Wright.

These days, Wright often considers her grandmother's life as she tries to juggle her own roles as daughter, aunt, godmother, chief executive, and community leader. Like her famous aunt, children's advocate Marian Wright Edelman, Wright views the children of Harlem as the key to its future.

"Kids need to see their options and the kids in Harlem haven't seen the full range of options that are before them. There were no investment bankers in Bennettsville, but I was grounded in confidence," she said.

And as Maggie Wright helped build her community in the 1940s, her granddaughter is trying to do the same for Harlem. She sees Carver as a community role model that can unlock the mysteries of money and encourage fiscal responsibility by the residents as Harlem undergoes a massive renaissance that brings new businesses and opportunities to its streets.

"Her whole life was mission. She's very hard to live up to. It's a blessing and a burden," Wright said with a tired smile.

But when she's feeling that burden, chances are "How Great Thou Art" will suddenly start playing somewhere nearby and, like her grandmother, she'll carry on.

CHAPTER TWO

From the Champions of Friends & Family

FRIENDSHIP

A good friend is a tower of strength;
to find one is to find a treasure.
—BEN SIRACH: Ecclesiasticus 6:14

Emotional support nurtures children mentally in much the same way healthy foods nurture them physically. How children play in preschool—whether they are rewarded for good sportsmanship or disciplined for behaving badly—how many times they are comforted when their feelings are hurt, or when they skin their knees on the playground, all have an impact on the adults they become. In many ways, children are like pearls. Although they all have the potential to become priceless, their environment has a direct impact on their development, and the type of pearl they will become. Will they become spherical or teardrop shaped? A beautiful rose or an exotic black? Or, will they be a more common white, but with a less than symmetrical, an abnormal shape?

And, if they are different from the rest of the children, will their differences be highly valued or misunderstood? In the case of children, the most important environmental influences encourage intellectual, moral, and physical growth. And, because not all children have families who can guarantee that these conditions are always available, it is important to realize that friends can encourage this development much in the same way as cultured pearls are grown. They can plant the seed from which the pearl will develop.

EMOTIONAL SUPPORT NURTURES CHILDREN MENTALLY AS HEALTHY FOODS NURTURE THEM PHYSICALLY.

Soon after joining the Albany *Times Union* as an office boy, I left the paper to serve in the United States Navy during the Korean conflict. Upon graduation from the radio training school I was sent to, I was assigned to the USS Recovery, a rescue and salvage vessel anchored at the Brooklyn Navy yard, only 150 miles from my Albany hometown.

As the ship had not moved in seven years, I was told I could expect a land-based tenure for my remaining naval service. However, less than an hour after I stepped aboard, the ship gave out the three-toot signal indicating it was leaving the dock for sea. My shipmates were cheered by the idea of actual sea duty, but I was grim about the notion of bouncing around a vast ocean for the next few years, having little to entertain myself with.

Assigned to my duty station on the bridge of the ship, where the radio shack was located, I approached my sea-bound assignment with distress and confusion. Also assigned by random drawing to my bunk, a slim strip of canvas just wide enough for an average-sized body, I found myself in the middle between an "upper" and "lower." The shipmate assigned the bunk above me was also, I noticed, one of the sailors working on the bridge of the ship. His name was Bob Myers. As we began to get to know each other, he told me he had joined the Navy after graduating from New York University with an honors degree in English Literature. Bob told me he chose to be an enlisted man rather than the officer his college background entitled him to because he wanted to taste the life of a team member, rather than a team official.

THE SECOND LOCKER WAS FILLED WITH THE CLASSICS—BLAKE, MILTON, HOMER, SHAKESPEARE.

Bob had negotiated for two lockers near our bunks and the second, I came to see, was filled with all the classics—books of Blake, Milton, Homer, Shakespeare, and what seemed to be every book in the Modern Library series.

With my learning-deprived foster-home background and truly minimal devotion to school or intellect, it seemed very natural and honest to tell Bob—as he opened that personal library he had jammed in his tiny locker—that I had never read a complete book. Instead of looking down his nose from his top bunk at me, Bob took it upon himself to educate me. For reasons unknown to me, Bob told me that he would adopt me as a student if I would be genuinely open to learning. Thus began my education abroad.

Bob would have me read one of the great novels, and then follow up with hours of fascinating time talking with me about character development, plot nuance, and the writing style of each great work's author. I had no idea where I was going with the information Bob gave me—I just knew that I enjoyed his teaching. He introduced me to worlds and people far removed from my previous experiences. He taught me how to let the author guide my imagination. He gave me a place to start and inspired me to do something more with the structure my social worker, Mae Morse, had years earlier helped me design. Bob illuminated my perspective through countless classic books and taught me to revere the unique gift an author can provide a reader. By the time I left the USS Recovery, I had the privilege of receiving a passionate guided tour through a vast collection of many of the world's greatest tomes.

When I returned from Navy service—inspired by my shipmate, Bob Myers, adopting me and guiding me to read all the great classic novels—I nervously thought about attending college for the first time. It is common for foster care kids to drift through school since often there is no force to encourage, guide, or even be interested in grades, homework, and so on. Foster care kids so often have all their intellectual and emotional energy so focused on not being pushed away from yet another foster family that little energy is left for schoolwork. Not unlike so many foster care kids, I had been wholly inattentive to school and had barely graduated from high school. Given that earlier reality, my appetite to apply to college was dampened by the sure fact that my high school grades were so poor they could be a barrier to college acceptance.

As so often happens in one's life, when you share your challenge with someone they can be the source of that "boost" you need to overcome your hurdle. I shared my burden with my girlfriend at the time (now my bride of over forty years) and she quietly contacted the Franciscan priests she had met while singing in their Siena College musical shows, and intervened on my behalf. They agreed to accept me on probation.

Although it thrilled me to walk into an actual college course and sense I could begin to reflect academic achievement as an English major, knowing my girlfriend's intervention was the only reason I could do so made me feel inadequate among the other students who, I assumed, had been accepted without question or probation. I was nervous and uncertain. Although I knew I had some advantage for English literature courses, I was petrified by the prospect of math, science, and language courses. That nervousness was with me for every single class in that first semester. It caused me to work with more diligence, more intensity, more fear of failure. And when my first test papers came back to me in each class, I saw those high grades affirming that simple hard work and commitment could overcome my weaknesses in those classes. For the first time in that college I had a sense of confidence, a sense of "I can do this," and a sense of excelling. It only took the combination of my own mental conviction and the grade endorsement of the professors in each class to lubricate my way to the dean's list. Once my name appeared on that list, I set aside uncertainty of my own college prospects and set sail for a learning journey. I had moved from personal, internal self-doubt to a conviction that I could do this and do it well. That conviction became a beacon for my life and my career. What had initially been only a seed planted by Bob Meyers ultimately became a pearl nurtured by my girlfriend and finally lifted me to a permanent new sense of my possibilities.

> FOR THE FIRST TIME, I HAD A SENSE OF CONFIDENCE, A SENSE OF "I CAN DO THIS," AND A SENSE OF EXCELLING.

Pearls of opportunity

by Aubrey Webb

Even lying beneath the shadow of that old Ford wasn't much protection *from the mid-afternoon July heat of Texas. Another Saturday night of drag racing had once again stripped transmission gears and I was out to best my record of seventeen minutes for installing a gearbox, obtained that morning from the local wrecking yard for twenty-five bucks.*

"Aubrey, we missed you this morning," a voice from above me said. The voice was that of Cecil Bunch, a Church of Christ minister, who for some reason thought I was worth saving. Cecil, as he insisted I call him, often stopped by—usually when I was working on my car. Often he would join me under the hood and offer his thoughts on the current problem. Today, however, was another first for our relationship as he threw a blanket under the car, rolled up the sleeves on his white shirt, and slid underneath. "Cecil," I said, "you are going to ruin your clothes." "Not if I'm careful," he said, "Now, what can I do to help?"

I had met Cecil Bunch months earlier in front of his church, following his Sunday morning sermon. I was a visitor, invited by a young lady who had caught my eye. She and her family were "church-goers," as they say. Her father was a Deacon and

any suitor of his daughter had better have some religion. I said I was Baptist.

I began to attend services regularly—Sunday school, Sunday morning service, Sunday night service, and Wednesday evening service. Cecil thought I was serious about religion. He began to encourage me to participate in other ways—be baptized in the church, teach Sunday school, lead the congregation in prayer. "Cecil," I would say, "I am not the person you think I am. I believe in God but I can't be the kind of person you want me to be." "It's not what I want," he would say, "it's what God wants. You can

CECIL THOUGHT I WAS SERIOUS ABOUT RELIGION, AND BEGAN TO ENCOURAGE ME.

be a leader and what better way to be a leader than to lead people along the path God would have them follow?" This talk scared me and I began to skip most services. Cecil stepped up his visits to my house. He was persuasive and I did miss

that young lady. Then one Monday night, Cecil and I had been talking and were headed for the church when he told me he had called my girlfriend and asked that she and her parents meet us there for a private baptism. He had won.

The next Sunday was Easter and I was to lead the congregation in prayer before Cecil took to his pulpit. I'll never forget the silence I heard as my lips moved close to the microphone, or the sound of my voice echoing through the public address system

to a gathering of more than six hundred people. I'll also never forget how powerful I felt. I found myself deviating from my prepared words. I was ad-libbing. I did not want to sit down. These people were in my control. I had them in the palm of my hand.

Over the next several months, I was in front of the congregation at every opportunity. Following the services men would shake my hand and pat me on the back. Little old ladies would hold my hand and tell me how much they enjoyed my

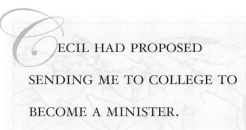

CECIL HAD PROPOSED SENDING ME TO COLLEGE TO BECOME A MINISTER.

prayer. I was still riding the euphoria train when reality looked me squarely in the eye.

Cecil and I were sitting on my front porch. He had come with a proposal that had left me shaky. I was staring at the ground while the little angel on my right shoulder and the little devil on my left shoulder were firing questions at each other.

This Church of Christ minister believed in me so much that he had sold the Deacons, the church's board of directors, on doing something they had not done before. Cecil had proposed sending me to a two-year college that would teach me to become a minister. The Deacons had approved paying all expenses as well as a salary for the two-year period. I was moved. I was speechless. I finally managed to tell him I would think about it, but I knew in my heart that I could not accept the offer.

Later the debate would sound like our earlier sessions: "I am not the person you think I am. I cannot be the person you or God want me to be—at least not now. Hopefully I can be that person at some time in the future."

"Cecil," I said, "if you insist on ruining your clothes, hand me the seven-sixteenths inch wrench." It would be the last time we worked on my car. He had come to tell me that he was moving, to take on new work with a new congregation.

Cecil Bunch changed my life. He forced me to look deep inside myself, to accept what was there, but also to know that it was not all bad. He made me believe that I had some leadership abilities. I will never forget that Church of Christ minister, who was also a pretty good mechanic.

FAMILY

*As the family goes, so goes the nation and
so goes the whole world in which we live.*
—POPE JOHN PAUL II

It takes a village. A couple of years ago this saying came under fire for many reasons—primarily because many of those opposed to it asserted that if each family took care of its own children, the United States would have fewer problems with the youth of its nation. Unfortunately, as was my case when growing up, circumstances occur during which many children do suffer and do not have all of their needs met by their family. It would be nice if every family around the world had the option to let the curve balls life throws them pass on by, but that is not the reality.

While doing research for *Every Child Deserves a Champion*, I came across quite a few profiles praising and detailing the efforts of individuals who have embraced the "It takes a village" mentality. I read about Father Gregory Boyle, a Jesuit priest who worked with current and former East Los Angeles gang members for years. I read about the more than seventy funerals he officiated. And I read about what he's done to give

THANKFULLY THERE ARE MANY INDIVIDUALS WHO HAVE DEVOTED THEIR LIVES TO CHAMPIONING CHILDREN.

former gang members and ex-convicts jobs—fresh starts and cycle-breaking opportunities that benefit their community. I read about his "Jobs not Jails" motto and the "Homeboy Industries," an organization he founded that provides job training. I also read about the efforts of such groups as Save the Children and UNICEF, and about all the work that is still waiting to be done, despite the efforts of these groups and individuals such as Father Boyle.

Thankfully, there are many individuals who have devoted their lives to championing children, despite the ups and downs associated with such a commitment. They continue their efforts to take care of "their village."

It Takes a Village

by Barb Fenster

I WAS A JOURNALIST, PRODUCING DOCUMENTARIES, WHEN I MET THE BOY WHO CHANGED *my life.*

I had taken my ten-year-old son to the movies one Saturday afternoon when my husband had to work. Sitting all alone in front of us was a tow-headed boy about my son's age. During the movie, the boy kept turning around to look at us.

When the show ended, my son headed to the bathroom while I waited in the lobby. The boy who'd been sitting in front of us came and, with a big smile, said, "Hi!" I "Hi-ed" him back. He asked if the boy with me was my son, and I said he was. The boy commented that it looked as though we were having a good time together. He asked if we did things together very often. I began thinking this was a very peculiar conversation to be having with a boy, but I gamely answered that, yes, we really enjoyed each other and did things together as often as we could.

The boy then asked if I had other children. Wanting to see where the conversation would go, I answered that I had only my son. That answer seemed to light up the boy, who promptly asked if I'd like to have more children. With a little stammering, I told him that we hadn't decided and asked him why he wanted to know.

The boy just looked at me for a moment. "You looked like a really nice Mom, and your son looks happy. I'm a foster kid and the family I'm staying with is moving, so I have to go to another family. My social worker says I may have to go to live in a group home if they can't find a family who will take me, and that really scares me. I wondered if you'd like to take me. I could be your foster son."

I was stunned.

I told him that I had to talk to my husband, then wrote down his name and phone number and told him that I would call him.

The next morning, in my most "no-nonsense" journalistic manner, I called the state Division of Children and Family Services and asked how it came to be that a child was trying to procure his own foster family. The social worker explained the harsh realities of foster care. Because of a critical lack of foster and adoptive families, she said, children often tried to find their own. When no home could be found for a child, there was little choice but to let the child stay overnight in the basement of the social service agency. Many of the older children hated this so much, that they chose to live on the streets.

I MAY HAVE TO LIVE IN A GROUP HOME IF THEY CAN'T FIND A FAMILY FOR ME.

When I asked why this was happening, the social worker said that few people seemed to care about these children, fewer were willing to take responsibility for them, and the state's budget for services was criminally small.

I asked about my boy and was told they'd look into the situation.

Several days later I called back, only to be told that because I was not a social worker, I could not access any information about my boy, and if I wanted to become a foster parent, they could see if the boy was still around after the three to six months it takes to get licensed.

I CALLED THE NUMBER THE BOY HAD GIVEN ME, BUT IT WAS TOO LATE.

I called the number my boy had given me, only to find out that it was too late. His family had moved and the boy was lost in the system.

The next week I convinced my television management to do a documentary about foster care. We aired three hours of commercial-free television about children lost in the foster care system and won a desktop full of awards for it.

But, it wasn't enough.

I had to get just one child out of the system.

My husband and I became foster parents. We adopted two children—a special *needs toddler boy and later, a ten-year-old girl. These children, and the experiences we've had with them, have reshaped my life. I left television to become a public relations/community outreach specialist working in foster care.*

Everything about my life changed because of a conversation I had with a boy. My family was altered forever. My professional life has turned upside down and with it, I have a new passion, a calling, to accomplish in my life. I am dedicated to making life better for the children in foster care.

I feel grateful to that boy for how profoundly he touched me and changed my life in wonderful ways. I also feel sorrow that after the tremendous gift he gave me, I couldn't help him. To this day, fourteen years later, I worry about what happened to him.

ROLE MODEL

Children have never been good at listening to their elders,
but they have never failed to imitate them.
—JAMES BALDWIN

Imitation is often said to be the greatest form of flattery. Toddlers often follow their older siblings around, who, in turn, often assume Mommy and Daddy's roles with them. The children look up the ladder for advice. And, as many parents who have had their children repeat a four-letter word or an off-color joke (which he or she doesn't usually understand) in front of guests can attest, there is no rhyme or reason to the little "treasures" children decide to imitate. Because of this, it is especially important to set a good example for them to follow—to give them an adaptable pattern that will help clothe them for every life experience. For me, an early pattern to follow was fashioned by Manny Kripps.

My first job after Margaret Mahoney's affirmation-intense office boy position was as a classified advertising salesman. This was a new frontier, requiring new baby steps as I faced the individual test of being a salesman dealing one on one with a customer. I was seventeen, with a baby face that made me look even younger. Surrounded by long-term experienced sales pros, I was so very intimidated by their comfortable excellence and my inexperience. Manny Kripps immediately took me under his wing to counsel me in the ways of what he called "customer royalty."

HE SERVED EACH CUSTOMER WITH A TAILORED EXCELLENCE, TREATING THEM AS ROYALTY.

He would take me to ride with him each Monday to simply observe his commitment to serve each customer with a tailored excellence. After each sales call he would tell me about the customer's family, hobbies, concerns, and business history—all learned by the simple mechanism of genuine interest and gentle questions from Manny to each customer. As I observed the marvelous relationships he developed by simply treating each individual as "royalty," I was inspired to "be like Manny" with every new client I was privileged to serve.

Very soon all my apprehensions faded and I could not wait for the next customer to become one of my living library of royalty. That attribute of genuine interest in others—asking gentle questions and being aware of the other person's needs/desires—became a fundamental platform as my career expanded. Whether the "customer" was one of our several thousand employee/colleagues, a single reader complaining about late newspaper delivery, or an advertiser running just a two-line classified ad, all were royalty in my mindset, and all were given the best I had to deliver.

Manny Kripps guided those baby steps. His early guidance became the pattern for almost every step that followed in my life.

He clothed me for life
by Faith Cooley Hesselgesser

I LIE ON THE FLOOR IN HIS WALK-IN CLOSET, STARING UP AT THE CLOTHES, SMELLING THE *stagnant air and the scent of someone not there. The clothes are methodically arranged—long-sleeved shirts, short-sleeved shirts, trousers, jackets, shoes, belts, and ties lining the wall like markings on a runway, with everything neat and in its place.*

My eyes wander through the long-sleeved shirts and rest on a corduroy burgundy shirt. It was a present, given to my father a couple of years ago, during the Christmas of my younger sister's engagement. During a quiet moment late in the

evening that holiday season, I sat with my father while he was wearing this shirt. He was sitting at the breakfast table drinking his usual cup of coffee and smoking a ciga-rette. We had had so many chats at that table, but that night he was particularly con-tent and pleased with my sister's choice. The last of his six children was taken care of.

Then there are the numerous short-sleeved cotton shirts. They look worse for the wear and tear. How many times had I returned from a hot Texas shopping spree to open the garage door and see him there, sitting high on his chair in his workshop, painstakingly piecing together another radio-controlled airplane? As I touch each one of these shirts, I can see their proud banners of stain, each marking a new addition to my father's air force. The volume of shirts speaks quietly to me of the number of days spent in this pastime.

The good trousers are segregated from the work trousers. My father was an inspector for Exxon. All through my childhood years he wore work clothes—heavy dark-green pants and shirts. I remember how his hair tonic smelled as I stood on the curb in my nightgown and kissed him goodbye as he left for work. My mother, sister, and I would wave until he was out of sight. During one visit home from college, I saw him leave for work. It was during his last few years of work, when he had a desk job. He looked awkward in his blue jacket, striped tie, and white shirt.

The cashmere jacket is as soft as butter. The color is a rich gray—a testament to my mother's desire to spiff him up when they went out. He wore that jacket the night

my mother debuted her new mink jacket—a mink purchased with money he had squirreled away over the years from his "allowance." He was not one for showing his emotions, but that night he and my mother looked so happy, so in synch, so together. He was half of a marriage to be envied.

His blue jeans hang on a hook next to the door of the closet—new blue jeans I had bought him just two weeks before. He had lost weight during his radiation treatments and his old jeans were almost hanging around his knees despite the belt. I bought him the new ones so he would not be arrested for exposure. He put the jeans on and "copped" a pose straight out of GQ. He wiggled around and "copped" another pose. I knew he was not feeling well and was doing it for me, but the pants fit.

The shoes are last. There is no more personal piece of clothing than a shoe—a shoe with the perfect and unique imprint of the wearer, and which can not be filled or walked in ever again.

And, while lying here on the closet floor my heart breaks into a million pieces. Somehow, I do not believe that he is gone, his smells and spirit are everywhere. But in looking at his clothes, I realize that my father clothed me for life.

LOVE

And in the end the love you take
is equal to the love you make.
—JOHN LENNON & PAUL MCCARTNEY

L ove. It has been the subject of countless songs and poems, described as everything from a "red red rose that's newly sprung in June" to a "conquerer of all." It has been the cause of such legendary battles as that begun over the renowned Helen of Troy, as well as an impetus for peace. And, for children around the world, it has been a sign of hope. Mother Teresa once said, "The hunger for love is much more difficult to remove than the hunger for bread." She was right. Waking up to love is like waking up to a sunny, worry-free, spring day—fresh, bursting with the promise of new life and possibilities. In my opinion, the only thing I can think of that is better than receiving love is giving love—especially when children are concerned.

Around the world there are children who are falling victim to war and famine. And, in the United States alone, there are children born every day to parents who for a variety of reasons are not equipped to take care of them. Many of these children, such as the young boy mentioned earlier by Barb Fenster, become lost in the foster system, continually at a loss for love. But for the lucky ones, there are couples such as Charles and Gayle Lichtman, and Jeff and K'Lin Noble, who are bursting with the precious emotion of love, and who want nothing more than to share it.

GIFT OF LOVE
by Charles Lichtman

DOCTORS COULD NEVER EXPLAIN WHY MY WIFE, GAYLE, AND I COULD NOT HAVE *children. In the late 1980s, we saw the top fertility specialists and tried every procedure that was suggested.*

During this time, I had a great-uncle, Sam Klein, who we called by his Hungarian name, Sandor. Uncle Sandor was a wonderful person with a big toothy smile for everyone, and someone who I had always felt a special connection to. Because of this connection, I visited him as often as possible at his tiny apartment in Miami Beach, where we would spend hours talking about everything, and often nothing at all.

One of the topics that came up during one of our visits dealt with the reason Gayle and I did not have children. Frankly, it was not a subject I felt like going into great detail about with my ninety-something-year-old uncle. Nevertheless, anyone who knew Uncle Sandor knows that he was not a guy who took no as an answer. So, under the pressure of trying not to offend him, and not being able to escape from his apartment until I told him every detail, I told him of our experiences with the fertility doctors and their test results.

Not long after this conversation, Gayle and I received a surprise telephone call from a rabbi who told us he was calling at Uncle Sandor's request. The gist of what this man of the cloth told us was that the doctors didn't know what they were talking about, but he did, and we had better listen to him if we wanted to have children. Gayle was given strict instructions to follow, which restricted her from driving and from going to work. She was to stay home and lie in bed all day long. There were about five other similar commandments hardly practical for this modern age, which, needless to say,

WE THANKED UNCLE SANDOR FOR HIS TRUE CONCERN.

we did not take too seriously. Although we never told this to Uncle Sandor, we thanked him for his true concern.

At about this same time, Gayle and I had concluded that we might not have kids together through natural means, so we visited an adoption agency. The meeting was distressing. The lawyer told us we would definitely qualify as adoptive parents, but because there was such a shortage of babies available for adoption, we should be prepared to have a long wait before we would get a baby—perhaps two years, a little less if we were lucky.

*W*E MIGHT NOT HAVE KIDS TOGETHER THROUGH NATURAL MEANS.

Within days after our visit to the lawyer, Uncle Sandor became ill. He passed on about two weeks later. As I drove to the gravesite the day of his funeral with my cousin, Kathi, we talked about the celebration of Sandor's life, rather than the loss of it. As is customary in Jewish funerals, at the conclusion of the burial, as we were driving out of the cemetery, we stopped near the exit gate to wash our hands. Over ten years later, I still remember the exact words I said as Kathi stood next to me and I looked up to the skies. "Uncle Sandor, if you ever had any connections, use them for me now."

We left the cemetery immediately afterwards, having said our goodbyes to Sandor at about 1:00 P.M. Continuing the Jewish tradition, the whole family went back to his apartment for a light meal and Shiva, and I stayed with the family until about

4:00 P.M. When I arrived home the first thing I did was check the telephone answering machine. To my complete shock, waiting for me was a message from the adoption lawyer, placed at about 1:30 P.M., advising that although she knew she just told us two weeks earlier that we'd have a long wait, a very unusual adoptive situation had just presented itself. She instinctively felt she had a baby who would be an absolutely perfect match for us. And she was.

Brooke Alexandra was born July 19, 1989, with blonde hair and blue eyes, just like Gayle's. She came from a birth mother who grew up in Indiana within ten

NOTHING WILL EVER CONVINCE ME THAT SHE WASN'T SENT TO US.

miles of where I did. I guess all parents feel this way, but Brooke has really been a special child since the day she was born. She is a combination of beauty, intelligence, and sensitivity that belies her youth. While I'm not a religious person and have never given a lot of thought as to what lies beyond death, nothing will ever convince me that Brooke wasn't sent to us by Uncle Sandor.

Two years later, we were blessed again with the adoptive birth of our second daughter, Jordan Nicole, who is equally as special as Brooke is. Amazingly, Jordan has all her sister's finest qualities, but remains her own person, with her own unique and

captivating personality. The two girls are inseparable and somehow I cannot help but think they were meant to be together. Many people say Brooke looks like Gayle and Jordan looks like me. Clearly, they both have taken on significant pieces of both of our personalities.

It is really simple. If the greatest gift in life is children, then Gayle and I were given the most generous gifts imaginable—our children. Uncle Sandor was indeed a champion for us all in his spirit advocacy, which resulted in the adoption of our two lovely treasures—our daughters.

Our little angels

by Jeff Noble

K'Lin and I had been married for five years when we decided we wanted to have a child. We thought that all we had to do was want children and there would be no problem. Unfortunately, that was not the way it turned out.

We soon realized traditional pregnancy was not going to be for us. Over the next five years, we were tested by doctors and had several in-vitro/insemination procedures. Every year as K'Lin's birthday approached, I would ask her, "What do you want for your birthday?" And, she would always reply, "A baby." That answer was always tough for me to handle. As a husband, I wanted to fix the problem and come up with a solution to resolve the situation. But, it was not that simple.

We would spend hours praying for a child. Many of our friends and family members began praying for us as well. Then one day in early fall, we received a call from a friend of ours in Europe. She told us about a niece in the United States who was expecting and wondered if we would consider adopting not one, but two babies—twins. She told us that she and her niece had been e-mailing each other and laboring over how to handle the situation. Her niece thought about both abortion and adoption and did not know what to do. The aunt talked her into adoption by giving her the name of a couple who would love the children. K'Lin and I turned out to be the couple.

Once we made contact with the birth mother, we found out that the children were boys and their due date was mid-November. Our physician informed us that twins could come early. Our attorney told us to expect anything with an adoption process. They were both right. Our attorney called us to his office one day and said that the birth mother had gone in for a checkup and her doctor decided to take the infants

K'LIN FINALLY RECEIVED HER BIRTHDAY WISH— CHILDREN.

early because one was out of the fetal sack. What happened next was truly God-sent— the boys were born on K'Lin's birthday. She finally received her birthday wish.

A few months after the boys were born and home with us, we noticed that the smaller twin was developing much slower than the other. We took him to several doctors and he was diagnosed with cerebral palsy. As any parents would be, we were crushed, but we quickly realized we should approach this setback aggressively. The palsy was mild and the doctors felt it would not keep our son from having a full independent life. He started therapy at eighteen months and began walking on his own with the aid of a walker.

K'Lin and I are both thankful for so many things we previously took for granted—our health, mobility, speech, and the knowledge of what it is like to be handicapped. People with disabilities are the true heroes in life. They overcome so much in order to do the simple everyday things. We have been blessed by the gifts of our children—our heroes. Every day with them is better than the day before.

PATIENCE

Patience and the mulberry leaf
becomes a silk gown.
—CHINESE PROVERB

We are only given what we have the capacity to handle. On more than one occasion I have heard this said to, or by, family, friends, and colleagues who are experiencing trying times. Although it is easy to verbalize, it is often harder to accept. When my daughter Marsha was diagnosed with childhood cancer at the tender age of five, my wife and I often asked ourselves why this was happening. How could we make it through this? And, when Marsha had one of her legs amputated when she was only fourteen years old, I remember the emotions flowing through me as I signed the papers at the hospital, giving my permission for the procedure to be done.

At the time, even though I knew our family was strong enough to get through this, I still didn't know how we would. The lesson I learned from this was patience. Combined with hope, the greatest resource we employed was patience. As I grew professionally, I carried this lesson from my personal life with me. Patience became one of the greatest tools I employed in working with colleagues.

PATIENCE BECAME ONE OF THE GREATEST TOOLS I USED IN WORKING WITH COLLEAGUES.

When I became publisher of the Albany *Times Union*, the inherited Advertising Director was sluggish and not furnishing the leadership or creativity his staff deserved. He had become what I called a "shelf case"— someone who merely functioned in the executive role rather than excelled. It was as if he had chosen to put himself on the shelf and hope he could simply rest there. Shelf cases of problem employee colleagues always bring a certain toxicity to those around them—it is a situation not to be permitted.

I chose to have several probing sessions with the executive until he revealed that he was struggling with a severely alcoholic wife and it had just stopped him in his tracks. He agreed that he had indeed become a shelf case. Remembering my own family's trials with my daughter Marsha's illnesses, I worked with him to find an Alcoholics Anonymous group near his home that he could persuade his wife to access.

We also agreed that his role as Ad Director was too central to let him just drift along. I created a new Community Relations Director position for him with the understanding we would both evaluate his progress for six months and, if this arrangement was not productive for us both, we would work out a severance plan. In the end he was superb in the new position, his wife made progress, and the Albany *Times Union* preserved the value of the long-term investment we had in him.

Shelf cases seem always to dampen the progress of an organization, a family, and a life. However, if one takes the time to get beneath the surface of the problem and examine the whole person, a resolution can be found that benefits all. In those special situations, you become a champion for the other by causing them to see how unwise their choices and conduct may be. It is not a role that you might choose easily, but by employing the patience needed to endure the ups and downs, it is a role that brings extreme satisfaction when the end result is fair to all.

> WITH PATIENCE, A RESOLUTION CAN BE FOUND THAT BENEFITS ALL.

Ups & downs

by Kenneth Lucas

Impatience. It has been my curse for years. It seemed as though whatever the circumstance—personal or professional—impatience drove my judgement. So much so, in fact, that I was often found to be quick tempered and "short" with people. Because of my impatience, I was also guilty of not listening to people. This character flaw got to be so bad that I found myself traveling through life and not enjoying it. Then, one summer, a magical thing happened. I met someone who would have a profound impact on my life.

Ken Whitten is a man of impeccable integrity, with a zest for people unlike any person I have ever met. Ken and I share a common bond—our love for baseball. As a result, we began our friendship by coaching our sons' little league baseball team. During those first few weeks of practice I noticed that Ken was enjoying it a lot more than I. He seemed to have a connection with these fifteen-year-old boys that I was very envious of. It took me a while to realize that what Ken was teaching these young men wasn't baseball (although he is an excellent baseball coach), it was life—how to enjoy your teammates, how to depend on them, and more importantly, how to love them.

Now comes the tricky part. Ken finally reached me through my son. You see,

Ken Whitten is the pastor at Idlewild Baptist Church in Tampa. My son, along with his friends, began going to church every Sunday morning. While this, in itself, is not a major accomplishment, what happened during the next year is something I will never forget.

Our son began to transform into a young man whom any father would be proud of. His friendships were deep and built on high moral and religious fiber. He seemed to have that same zest for life that Ken Whitten has. I began admiring my son and wishing I was like him. Then, one Sunday, Jeff came home from church and informed me that a member of his baseball team had been killed in an auto accident the night before.

At the funeral the baseball team sat together. My wife and I were two rows back listening to a tearful Ken Whitten deliver a message about the young man who had been taken from us so early in life. I sat staring at my son, Jeff, thinking it could have been him. I began to cry as we bowed our heads in prayer. It was there that I began realizing why Ken Whitten and Jeff loved life so much; their patience with the "downs" helped make it easier for them to enjoy all of the "ups."

FAITH

With faith there are no questions:
without faith there are no answers.
—"THE CHOFETZ CHAIM"

Have you ever played the childhood game during which one person stands behind you, while you fall backwards, with complete faith that you will be caught in time? By putting your faith in the person standing behind you, you make the choice to fall into the unknown, with complete faith that you won't have a hard landing.

A couple of years ago a family friend, Lucille Cazzetto, found herself putting her faith in the care of complete strangers when she was diagnosed with breast cancer. On the day of her surgery, the nurse attending her asked if she had a history of high blood pressure. Lucille said she did not, but was told that her blood pressure was very high.

"What do you do when you are nervous?" the nurse asked her.

"I pray," she said.

A moment later another nurse arrived at the bedside to begin the IV. She was told what had transpired and began to pray with them. As Lucille's blood pressure returned to normal, her feelings became peaceful again. These two nurses, complete strangers, had caught Lucille when she began "to fall." They had championed the strength of her faith and helped to restore it in the success of her surgery.

As in Lucille's case, children of all ages are faced with tackling frightening challenges. And although some have a strong faith in their abilities, for those who begin to doubt the outcome of the situation they are in, having someone who can help catch them when their faith starts to fall can make all the difference.

The gift of faith
by Dorian Vallejo

My first blessing or stroke of good fortune was to be born into a family of *endless loving support. It was an atmosphere charged with the sense of personal reward that comes from honest hard work and a belief in oneself.*

My father had always been a symbol to me of what can be accomplished by

not allowing fear to impede or destroy one's dreams or goals. Originally from South America, he came to this country with a one-way ticket, very little money, and no understanding of the English language. The only things he possessed were his dreams to be an artist and an unwavering faith in his ability to accomplish that feat in one of the most competitive places in the world—New York City.

My birth, followed almost immediately by the birth of my sister, happened only a short time after his arrival in this country. One can imagine that this must have been

THE MAIN UNDERLYING IDEA EXPRESSED THAT AFTERNOON HAD BEEN ABOUT FAITH.

a time of incredible strain for him, having to support a family and still pursue his artistic ambitions. However, when I see photos from that time period, I see a happy man without any sign of stress. When I hear stories about those early days, they are always about a man who exploded with energy, whose very presence in a room was electric enough to spark things into happening. In a relatively short time, my father became one of the most eagerly sought after artists in New York and in this country. Now as I write this, his reputation is on a global scale.

As a child I can remember many visitors to our house seeking advice from my father regarding their artistic careers. I was seldom present during these meetings—not because I was not welcome but because, as a child, I had other interests to engage my *time. However, as the guests came rather often, from time to time I would sit patiently by my father's side, capturing bits and pieces of a conversation while I leafed through a visitor's portfolio. One day, at just such a meeting (I couldn't have been but seven or eight years old), I was stunned to hear one such person exclaim, "…but what if I put all this work and energy into my paintings and I still fail?!" My mouth fell open—I could not believe it! Hadn't he heard anything my father had said? What he lacked in the technical or mechanical ABC's of the craft could be learned.*

The main underlying idea expressed during their conversation that afternoon had been about faith—faith in one's ability to accomplish not only the task ahead of him, but any others that the future might bring. The idea of absolute and total faith in one's ability to accomplish his dreams was to be the single most important bit of knowledge given me early in life and patiently nurtured by my father, a man who has lived life as a shining example of that concept.

I am truly aware of how lucky I've been to have that special person as my father. To have his example before me enables me to set my own personal standards as high as I would like, and eagerly to look forward to the challenges life will offer me on my journey, every day and in the future.

TRUST

To be persuasive, one must be believable.
To be believable, we must be credible.
To be credible, we must be truthful.
—EDWARD R. MURROW

When I first had the privilege of becoming publisher of the Albany *Times Union*, I was most aware of the high tension level between the eleven unions representing employee colleagues. I also realized that strained relationships would only result in reluctant contributions by our 972 employee colleagues to our potential progress. Tensions were so great that, for example, if a member of management walked through the printers' workplace (the composing room) and said "Good morning," any printer who answered would be fined one hundred dollars by the union or, if they did not have the cash with them, sent home with pay reduced for the lost hours.

The chapter chairman had a particularly venomous mouth, and was constantly criticizing management. At the annual company steak-bake for all employees, I was introduced to his wife. Some weeks later I was doing our family grocery shopping when, pushing her basket toward me, came the chairman's wife. No sooner had I greeted her than she burst into tears. When she finally caught her breath she told me her husband had suffered a severe back injury, could only sit up for a few hours a day, and had entered into a deep depression sensing that he would never be able to return to work. She told me he could sit up for those few hours by use of a special orthopedic chair their doctor had furnished. I asked for the doctor's name and the next day called the doctor, and ordered another of those chairs to be put in our composing room. I called the chairman's home and told his wife that her husband could come to work for those few hours, serving as a proofreader sitting in the special chair. I then called the union president and told him we needed to work out an agreement that would allow the chairman to work less than the full shift required by the union contract. I told him I would sign an agreement stating that this would be nonprecedential and not influence their general union

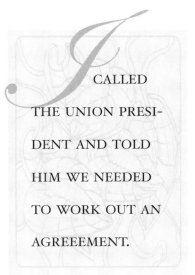

I CALLED THE UNION PRESIDENT AND TOLD HIM WE NEEDED TO WORK OUT AN AGREEEMENT.

rules. He refused, telling me that should the chapter chairman be brought to work for less than a full shift he would take the printers out on strike. A very serious situation indeed. Nevertheless, I called the chairman's wife and suggested she have the van used for wheelchairs bring her husband to the plant the next day.

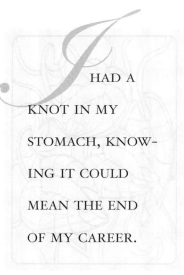

I HAD A KNOT IN MY STOMACH, KNOWING IT COULD MEAN THE END OF MY CAREER.

All the printers knew of the situation and the tension level was at a peak. When the chairman and his wife arrived at the plant, I took the wheelchair and pushed it through the plant door and up to the pneumatic doors of the composing room, where pressure on the rubber floor mat would open the doors automatically. I suggested to the chairman's wife that she give the final push to open the doors. As I walked away, I had a knot in my stomach, knowing that if the printers walked out in a protest, it could mean the end of my career as publisher.

I was some twenty feet away from the door when I heard the "swoosh" of the pneumatic door opening. The next sound was a roar of cheers from all those printers looking at the union chairman, in his wheelchair, now able to rejoin them in dignity as a worker, even though only a few hours a day. From that day forward any member of management could walk through the composing room and chat with the printers as individuals—not just as union members. That new bridge of trust permeated the entire newspaper plant from that day forward.

We each build "trust bridges" throughout our lives—whether with family, friends, workplace colleagues, or neighbors. The "planks" you choose determine the strength of the bridge. By treating each with individual dignity and value, you create something that will weather time—something that shows others they can trust and rely on the strength of the structures you have built. The following story by Cynthia Aponte, who grew up in the foster care system, shows how a strong bridge of love and trust can change a life for the better.

BRIDGING HAPPINESS

by Cynthia Aponte

I SPENT SEVEN YEARS IN A KINSHIP FOSTER HOME, BETWEEN THE AGES OF FIVE AND *twelve. During that time, I experienced a lot of emotional and physical abuse. Sometimes I believe that if I had spoken up, I would have had a happier childhood.*

While living with my kinship foster mother, I was rarely allowed to have fun and participate in recreational activities. At least once a month she would take the entire family out to the zoo, the park, or to the botanical gardens. She never allowed me to play; I would have to stand by her side. Think about it: the torture a kid feels watching others playing and having fun while she can't. When summer came, I also had to stay inside while other children played outside with their friends.

I didn't even look forward to my birthday because it was just like any other day. My foster mother wouldn't celebrate it, and when I received gifts from my birth parents, my foster mother would give them to her son or daughter.

It wasn't until my eldest sister left the foster home that I realized my foster mother's actions were wrong. I was young and really hadn't understood what was happening to me. When the caseworker asked how we were doing, I was too scared to say anything negative. I had already experienced emotional trauma the first time I was

taken from my home. I wasn't ready to go through more unknown changes in my life. But I was so unhappy, I ran away and was removed from the home. Little did I know how my life would change for the better.

At my new foster home I am allowed to enjoy life and its luxuries. On recreational days we enjoy ourselves. I am allowed to participate in the planning of all activities—AND—my birthday is celebrated and I receive all gifts. I have birthday parties and I can plan how I want my birthday to be celebrated. And, during disputes I am not physically or emotionally abused. I learned that we can resolve issues by talking and coming to a fair solution for all involved.

I cannot undo or go back to the lost years of my early childhood in my old foster home. But I learned from my mistake of not speaking up. It was at my new home that I learned how happy my life could have been had I spoken up sooner.

Spiritual Oasis

JUST DOWN THE STREET

by Robin Sidel

Six floors below her corner office and a few blocks south, Lisa Quiroz can practi-
cally see the spot on 44th Street where she used to go with her grandmother in search
of a culinary specialty. The two of them would make the long trek from Staten Island
to mid-town Manhattan—the immigrant grandmother who never left the house without make-up, stockings, and perfume, and the young Hispanic girl growing up in the
1970s as the odd one out in an Irish and Italian neighborhood.

"It was the only place where you could get corn tortillas in the city," said Quiroz.

Times certainly have changed.

As the publisher of Spanish-language *People* magazine, Quiroz is in the forefront of the Hispanic cultural revolution sweeping the country. From pop star Ricky Martin to the jars of salsa lining shelves in every American supermarket, the Latino influence has taken hold.

It wasn't always that way. Quiroz, the daughter of a Puerto Rican mother and Mexican father, was one of three minority children in her Catholic school. When she was only fourteen years old, an Italian boy told her that he couldn't date her because she was Puerto Rican.

QUIROZ IS IN THE FORE-FRONT OF THE HISPANIC CULTURAL REVOLUTION.

"Now, as an adult, I realize how unbelievably racist it was. It was a terrible environment. That's why it is so important to raise a kid with a sense of identity," she said.

Leonar Quiroz, her paternal grandmother, was an integral part in helping her establish that identity.

Orphaned at age eight, Leonor was fourteen years old and working as a maid for a minister in Pueblo, Mexico, when she was offered the chance to come to America with her employer's brother, who was a minister in Brooklyn. The young girl, who had grown up on a farm, boarded a train, and five days later arrived in New York. Once there, she learned to read and write English, and was introduced to theater, opera, and art by the minister and his cultured wife, whose granddaughter years later just happened to be singer and songwriter Joan Baez.

Leonar married and settled on Staten Island. Each day, she would put on a dress, stockings, make-up, and perfume, and take a bus, ferry, and subway to her factory job in Manhattan. When her two sons were in college, she would wash and iron their shirts every night so that no one would know that they each only had one shirt hanging in their closets.

"She taught me the value of hard work and she gave me tremendous self-confidence," Quiroz said.

> SHE TAUGHT ME THE VALUE OF HARD WORK AND SELF-CONFIDENCE.

Quiroz grew up with her grandmother living in her house—a home where Spanish was spoken, and native foods and music were commonplace.

When Quiroz was about ten, her grandmother, who was living with Quiroz's family, took her eldest grandchild on a trip to Mexico. Although she had often visited her mother's family in Puerto Rico, it was her first trip to her grandmother's homeland. For two months, grandmother and granddaughter traveled around the country.

"She instilled in me a strong sense of culture," Quiroz said.

And it was not only the culture of her heritage. It was her grandmother who took Quiroz to the museums of New York, her first off-Broadway show, and who gave her skating lessons at the ice rink in Rockefeller Center.

When she was fourteen years old, Quiroz's parents and siblings moved to Colorado for a temporary work assignment for her father. Quiroz wanted to go to high school in Staten Island, so she stayed behind, and lived with her grandmother.

Needless to say, their relationship grew even closer when it was just the two of them, especially when her father's job became more permanent. Quiroz began taking on more responsibilities in the house, paying the bills, and balancing the checkbook. And when her parents' relationship fell apart, it was her grandmother who continued to love her, support her, and encourage her.

SHE INSTILLED IN ME A STRONG SENSE OF CULTURE.

"She was an incredible anchor for me. When people are in bad relationships, they become very selfish. I was the focus of her world," Quiroz remembered.

The strong sense of self-worth instilled by her grandmother eventually led Quiroz to Harvard University, where she earned an undergraduate degree in sociology and a master's degree from Harvard Business School. She then got a job in the consumer marketing department of *Time* magazine.

But it was a trip back to elementary school that put Quiroz's career on a fast track. When returning to the classroom as part of a "Principal for a Day" program, Quiroz realized that her former teachers were still using the same teaching tools that were in place so many years before. She went back to Manhattan and created *Time for Kids*, a classroom news magazine for students in second through sixth grades.

THE STRONG SENSE OF SELF-WORTH EVENTUALLY LED TO HARVARD.

In 1997, Quiroz again returned to her roots—this time as the first publisher for *People* magazine's newest project—a Spanish-language edition. By then Quiroz's parents had divorced and her grandmother was living with her father in San Francisco. But their bond was still in place and Quiroz made certain that her aging grandmother shared in her success, knowing she would get a kick out of seeing the Hispanic business magazine that featured Lisa on the cover, and the little promotional items from *People En Español*.

Because she knows that not everyone has been as lucky to have a grandmother like hers, Quiroz today works hard at reaching out to young people, recruiting minority students for Harvard. "I tell them the importance of following your dreams, working hard, and thinking big."

CHAPTER THREE

A Whole New World of Champions

EXPLORATION

*I think at a child's birth, if a mother could ask a
fairy godmother to endow it with the most unusual gift,
that gift would be curiosity.*
—ELEANOR ROOSEVELT

Most children are like cats—curious about everything. They crawl into cupboards and pull all the pots and pans onto the kitchen floor so they have room to play inside. Many have been known to flush almost everything they can get their little hands on down the toilet, to see just how much the toilet can hold. And, some have even discovered new food units by storing their snacks in VCRs, under couches, and sometimes in Dad's shoes. They aren't being bad. Uncharted territory just happens to be the name of the game and they simply need to explore and test everything—and often everyone—to discover what works and what doesn't. Because of this, they also need someone who can be patient with them and who is willing to be a leader without giving away all the answers—someone who leads by supporting them from behind, allowing them to fall back and make mistakes they can learn from, rather than pulling them in all the right directions, and never letting them figure out new lessons for themselves. For me, such a leader was Frank J. Nigro.

Frank J. Nigro always described himself as a simple grocer. Indeed, when he rented his first compact corner grocery store on the corner of South Allen and Central Avenues, in Albany, New York, this description seemed generous, since he sold only fruits and vegetables in the modest store. However, Frank creatively merchandised everything from each stalk of celery to each apple in outdoor bins that brimmed with impeccably positioned displays.

THEY NEED SOMEONE WHO CAN BE PATIENT WITH THEM AND BE A LEADER WITHOUT GIVING AWAY ALL THE ANSWERS.

His dream was for his store, Albany Public Market, one day to be a full-fledged supermarket, in which he could let his merchandising flair roam. It was not long, indeed, before he managed a bank loan and opened a major full-service supermarket about one mile up the road from his first corner-stand store.

Within a few years, Frank opened several area supermarkets and Albany Public Market became the dominant grocery chain in the entire area. It was at this point of business maturity that he became a thread of life in my ever-developing personal tapestry.

At that time in the Albany area's media history, the Gannett corporation-owned *Knickerbocker News* was the dominant advertising vehicle for several merchandise categories. This included the grocery ads, in which the paper enjoyed a one hundred percent share of the field. There was no share in the morning *Times Union* where I worked. At the time, I was a classified advertising salesman, only recently married, and seeking a move to the display ad staff where the salary was higher. I proposed to our advertising director, Mark Collins, that he let me have a chance to handle the grocery advertising sales territory while I retained my classified ad job. No increase in salary, I proposed, unless I could produce some results in a reasonable time. He agreed, and I became a new retail ad salesman handling grocery accounts, with zero business.

I immersed myself in studying the grocery business and culling out small suggestions for any merchant to improve his business. The ads from the competing *Knickerbocker News* became my ammunition. I redesigned each ad, had it set in type, and delivered proofs to every grocery business as an example of how they might improve their advertising.

While I visited each grocer twice a week, I called on Albany Public Markets and Frank Nigro every single day. He was an impeccable man—medium in height, with shining hair slicked straight back, and a classic Italian face, including a roman nose any sculptor would be proud of.

Within two months, Frank Nigro called me aside, stared directly at me, hunched his shoulders, and announced that starting the next week he would be splitting his ten ad pages and giving five of those to the *Times Union*. Celebration! Because his stores were the food category leaders, all the other grocery stores followed his lead within a few weeks, and suddenly my *Times Union* had fifty-five percent of the grocery advertising. In fact, within two years our company acquired the competing *Knickerbocker News*. Their business went into irrevocable decline when they lost the grocery advertising.

HE ANNOUNCED THAT STARTING THE NEXT WEEK HE WOULD BE SPLITTING HIS ADVERTISING.

Because I continued to call on Frank every day with some new idea, we became very close. Within a few years there came an opportunity for me to apply for the retail advertising manager position at the newspaper. When I applied, I was told I was too young and would not be considered. Disappointed, I set off for my daily call on Frank Nigro. Because he knew me so well he could sense my slump and asked what was wrong. I explained that I had been turned down for the manager slot as being too young. "Not a problem," said Frank, "just go down today and quit." I told him I was married with a child and could not simply quit my job. He said, "You will not be out of a job, you will come to Albany Public Markets on Monday and become my advertising and promotion manager." I did just that.

Some six weeks later I received an invitation to lunch from the ad director of the *Times Union*. During lunch, the director, Roger Coryell, told me he had re-assessed my credentials and concluded that, although I was young, I was the right man for the retail ad manager position. I listened with my heart beating wildly, but gave no response. After lunch, I went to Frank Nigro's office. He looked up from his paperwork with a slight smile and said, "They offered you the job, didn't they?" I told him they had

ALL HE DID WAS TO OFFER "A PORT IN THE STORM" UNTIL THE NEWSPAPER EXEC-UTIVES "CAME TO THEIR SENSES."

but I did not comment, since I was now working for him. He looked at me and said, "Your destiny is to be in the newspaper business, not the grocery business. All I did in providing you this job was to offer you 'a port in the storm' until the newspaper exec-utives came to their senses."

A port in the storm. That phrase never left me as I returned to the newspaper and began a journey that would ultimately lead me to the helm of our company for twenty years. Frank J. Nigro, called FJN by his friends and associates, proved to be a compass assisting me as I navigated my life's direction. He led me by pointing out the variety of explorations available, leaving me to decide the one that best suited my preferred route.

Guiding lights
by Sister Patrice

Several years ago, at the request of one of our alums, I was asked to give a talk to the local Presbyterian's Women's Club. When I asked the alumna what she wanted me to talk about, she said, "Oh, anything you want… they don't know much about nuns, so talk about being a nun and about being a president of a college… anything." She did give one specific directive, though: "Begin with the story of when you were seven years old." The story she referred to was one I had told at the beginning of my inaugural address when I was installed as the president of Caldwell College.

"I'm speaking to you [I began my address] on the very spot where I played as a seven-year-old child. There was no building then (the Student Center where the ceremony was held was not built until 1970). It was fertile land that at one time had been farmed by the Sisters of Saint Dominic. Where I played was partially overgrown with trees… I spent three early grade school years at Mount Saint Dominic Academy board-ing school while my mother worked, returning home to Jersey City in the sixth grade. Then, after high school at St. Dominic Academy, I came back to Caldwell to enter the community of the Sisters of St. Dominic."

In my talk I went on to thank the sisters who took care of a frightened seven-year-old child, nurtured and empowered her, and finally, entrusted her with Caldwell College. A simple story—hardly the stuff of great spiritual journeys. But if my story has any value to anyone other than myself, maybe that value lies in its ordinariness, in its illustration of the slow working out of the will and ways of God in our ordi-nary everyday living. To be inaugurated president of a college on the very spot

I WENT ON TO THANK THE SISTERS WHO TOOK CARE OF ME AND EMPOWERED ME.

where I once played as a child is unusual but scarcely the stuff of great drama.

What the alumna didn't know when she asked me to tell the story is probably more indicative of the strange ways of God. That seven-year-old child who grew up to be a nun and president of Caldwell College was not even Catholic at the time, but was *actually baptized in Trinity Chapel, Church of Christ, in New York, and came to Mount Saint Dominic boarding school only because her mother happened to work with a very dear lady, a devout Catholic, who knew she needed someone to take care of a small child while she worked, and who suggested the Mount. Eventually, my Aunt Marie, as I called her, became my godmother when both my mother and I converted to Catholicism three years later.*

My aunt is dead now, but her influence in my life will never be forgotten. She was a true champion to me in my early years. Without her influence I would not have gone to Mount Saint Dominic and started on the path that would lead to conversion to Catholicism, an education in the Dominican tradition, entrance into the religious community, and a long career in education.

CONFIDENCE

Besides pride, loyalty, discipline, heart, and
mind, confidence is the key to all the locks.
—JOE PATERNO

When I first had the opportunity to meet Gene Robb, he was the publisher of the Albany *Times Union*. He was a gentle, but leathery presence. Integrity shone from him. I was a young ad salesman supporting a new family, and was going to school nights at Siena College to further my education; nothing glamorous—at least not to me. Gene, however, saw more.

Gene Robb was on the Board of Trustees at Siena College, and therefore received every publication the college printed, including the literary journal, *The Beverwyck*, which I had begun to publish small pieces in. One day, we were riding on the elevator at the paper when he turned to me and said, "I see an R. Danzig at Siena

College writing for *The Beverwyck.* Is that someone related to you?" I replied, "No, Mr. Robb. That is I. I go to Siena College at night." Our conversation ended there, but Gene Robb subsequently did something one might not be able to do today. Without my knowledge, he had my grades sent to him after every semester.

When I graduated from Siena College in 1962, Mr. Robb asked me to join him for breakfast one Saturday morning. He told me that it was his intention to retire from the publisher's position in 1974 and write editorials. It was over this breakfast that I learned he had been keeping an eye on me, studying me as it were, and having my grades sent to his office. He said, "I've concluded, at this time, that I would like you to be an optional candidate to succeed me someday. With that in mind, I am going to put you in a program where you'll go into the various disciplines of the newspaper. But, the deal will be, that whatever job you go into, if you can't cut it, you can't go back to the old job. You're not going to be a crown prince. You really must perform every assignment."

> THIS WAS A HALLMARK OF THE MAN WHO WOULD ALWAYS PUT THE EMPHASIS ON DOING THE RIGHT THING.

Although Gene Robb was providing me an opportunity, there was a high performance bar requirement. This was a hallmark of the man who would always put the emphasis on doing the right thing. Fortunately, when he offered me this opportunity to try new things, he also offered personal counsel that helped reinforce my ability to succeed. Long before he became publisher and chairman of *Parade* magazine, my close friend, Walter Anderson, went through a similar experience. His source of inspiration was the mother of a childhood friend. Her reinforcement of his self-worth and ability has stayed with him his entire life.

YOU CAN DO THIS

by Walter Anderson

BARRY WILLIAMS WAS MY BEST FRIEND WHEN I WAS GROWING UP IN WHITE PLAINS. *In many ways, our lives were completely different. He lived in a two-story clapboard house with a backyard; my family occupied a railroad flat in a tenement building. My home life was troubled; his seemed serene. He was black; I'm white. I dropped out of high school; he went on to Harvard. But what we had in common—what made all the difference in the world to me—was Barry's mother, Mrs. Williams.*

I didn't even know her first name. She was always Mrs. Williams, the tall, dignified school teacher across the street who was rearing three sons on her own.

Sometimes Mrs. Williams told us stories. "A long time ago, in the marsh coun-

try of England, there lived an orphan boy named Pip," she might say. "One bleak evening he was visiting the graves of his parents. The sky darkened, and the wind blew, and the boy, afraid, started crying. Suddenly a deep voice roared, 'Keep still or I'll cut your throat!' and a terrible figure rose from among the tombstones."

"Then what happened?" I asked, enthralled.

"If you'd like to know," she answered, smiling, "read the book Great Expectations, by Charles Dickens." She made me want to go to the library.

Other times Barry and I would be out in the driveway on a Saturday shooting hoops, and his mother would say, "Boys, could you come and give me a hand?" The next thing we knew, we would be helping her with a student she was tutoring. I felt proud that Mrs. Williams valued my help. I didn't realize until much later that by teaching someone else, Barry and I were learning too.

I WASN'T USED TO THIS KIND OF DISCIPLINE— OR ATTENTION.

Mrs. Williams made sure that Barry and his brothers did their homework, and if I happened to be visiting, she watched while I did mine. Usually Barry and I studied at the kitchen table. Mrs. Williams stayed nearby, in case we had a question. At home I lived in fear of my father's alcoholic rages, and I wasn't used to that kind of discipline—or attention.

Her favorite words of encouragement were "You can do this." I heard them often because I was impatient and easily frustrated. When a math problem refused to yield its secret or an essay had me confounded, I gave up and slammed my pencil on the table. Calmly, Mrs. Williams took a seat beside me and talked me through the assignment step-by-step. Something about her quiet reassurance, "You can do this, Walter," settled me down, and I managed to finish my work.

Barry and his brothers went to private schools—an expense that must have strained Mrs. Williams's budget—and she worried about the quality of my education. One day she took me to a local parochial school, had me tested, then persuaded my parents to let me change schools.

I attended for a while, but after an angry exchange with a teacher, I was told not to come back. Unperturbed, Mrs. Williams took me to another school, had me tested again, made sure I would receive the necessary financial assistance, then convinced my parents that it was important for my future. I made it through two grades in one year.

When we were ready for high school Barry applied to boarding schools. Mrs. Williams believed that would be the best thing for me as well; anything to get me away from the streets, where she saw too many kids getting into trouble. I was accepted into a prep school and again awarded a scholarship. But when I saw the other students—

kids in pressed shirts and blazers—all my old insecurities came rushing back. I could-n't do it. I entered the high school in town. A year and a half later, failing nearly every subject, I dropped out.

One of the hardest things I've ever had to do was tell Mrs. Williams. She gazed at me with her cool brown eyes and said nothing. "I'm going into the Marines," I said, shrugging. "I won't need high school."

"Okay, Walter." Her voice was quiet, resigned. "I don't agree with you, but you're old enough to make your own decisions."

Six months later, in the Marines, I realized how right she was. In three and a half years I would be out of the service, a twenty-one-year-old with no diploma. What sort of future would I have? Dear Lord, *I prayed,* please give me another chance.

The next morning, I went to the First Sergeant and said, "I want to go to school." The first step was to take an exam for a high school equivalency diploma. I must have done well, because after seeing my scores, the Marines enrolled me in a spe-cial electronics program.

Again I felt out of my league. Dear God, *I prayed,* let me pass just one course. *The instructor began his lecture. I started taking notes, but there was so much I didn't know; so much I was afraid I would never know.* There's no way I'll get through this class, *I thought, putting my pen down.* I should just walk out the door right now.

All at once I heard a familiar voice inside my head, warm and reassuring: "Don't give up Walter. You can do this." I wasn't so sure, but I owed it to Mrs. Williams—and to myself—to try. Taking a deep breath, I picked up my pen and concentrated on my instructor's lecture.

I graduated seventh in a class of twenty-four. It was the biggest thrill of my life. I can't wait to tell Mrs. Williams, *I thought. But by the time I made it back home the Williamses weren't living across the street anymore. They had moved and no one knew their new address.*

After the Marines I went on to receive my bachelor's degree. By the age of twenty-six I was well into a career in journalism. I became a newspaper editor and eventually editor-in-chief of Parade *magazine.*

Several years ago when I spoke at a dinner, I told the audience, "All the successful people I've known have one thing in common.

I GRADUATED SEVENTH IN A CLASS OF TWENTY-FOUR. IT WAS THE BIGGEST THRILL!

In their childhood there was someone who said, 'I believe in you.' For me, that was my best friend's mother, Mrs. Williams." It was gratifying to give her credit. Still, I longed to tell her how she had changed my life, to thank her for all she had done for me.

Some time later, I talked to Parade's *senior investigative reporter about Mrs. Williams. "I wish I could get in touch with her," I said.*

"I can find her," he declared.

A few days later he called. "Walter," he said, "Mrs. Williams lives a few miles away from you. She's retired from teaching now and Barry is a successful attorney."

Mrs. Williams and I had a reunion at my house. All I could do at first was thank her over and over again. Then the words spilled out in a rush, as I told her about everything I had accomplished, eager to make her proud. "I graduated college as valedictorian. Then I got into journalism and today I'm the editor-in-chief of a magazine."

She gave me a broad smile. "Of course, you are, Walter," she said, her voice as full of assurance as it had been so many years ago. Ilza Louise Berry Williams never doubted for a moment that I could accomplish anything I set my mind to. It just took me a while to believe it for myself.

REINFORCEMENT

When we are confident,
all we need is a little support.
—ANDRE LAURENDEAU

When publisher Gene Robb, my guiding hand at the Albany *Times Union*, died suddenly of a heart attack, I was privileged to succeed him. At the time, our newspaper operation was plagued with executive competition. I knew first hand from attending weekly management sessions that each jealously guarded its own departmental turf and bristled when any other manager suggested an area of opportunity in another's operation. The net effect, I observed, was a type of paralysis that allowed the company to function each day but inhibited any collective quest for new excellence, new horizons, new possibilities. I felt as if this circumstance would cause me to only be a referee attempting to settle petty disagreements rather than bringing a stimulus for creative new initiatives to pave our future. Not one of these executives was a force for progress in the collective purpose of the newspaper since all their concentration was on their own feet, as it were, in their own shoes exclusively. My personal frustration level was high.

After a few weeks of struggling with this unproductive reality of executive tensions, I reached out to a newspaper executive development resource, The American Press Institute, and sought their agreement to permit an executive to attend a two-week session in an area of responsibility different from their own. I was told no one had ever requested this and they would need to confer with the governing board since there was a risk of discomfort if, for example, an editor attended an advertising manager session, and vice versa. When they did finally concur, I sat down with each and all of the competing managers and told them they would be attending these several week sessions in each other's area of expertise. They would learn, I told them, to walk in the "other person's shoes." Reaction was universally negative, but off they went to the courses in New York City. Within just a few months of genuinely learning about the challenges of each other's specialty areas, they began

I SAT THEM DOWN AND TOLD THEM THEY WOULD LEARN TO "WALK IN THE OTHER PERSON'S SHOES."

a new language of insight, understanding, and co-operation. Within six months we had committees working collectively on "new horizons"—"fresh excellence" and an internal "cross-pollination" of employee colleagues so we could have a much broadened landscape of collective goals. That stepping into the other person's shoes changed the destiny of that business. Each of those executives simply had to learn to be a champion for the other.

You should always seek out ways to understand another person and, when the opportunity is there, be a champion for them. The following story, by Lynn Price, is one such example of how understanding and seeking to explore what another person is going through can be a "win-win" situation for all involved.

Endless support
by Lynn Price

"*She's not my sister! She's not my sister!*" *I exclaimed glaring at the nine-and-one-half-year-old, curly-headed girl standing before me. While I backed farther up against the wall behind me, hoping to disappear into another room, she slowly walked forward with her hand outstretched and a soft, sure smile on her face.*

At eight years old, I found out my parents weren't really my parents. They

were my foster parents. My father had abandoned the family when I was eight months old. My mother had a nervous breakdown and was placed in an institution. No one in the extended family could take care of me, so I was placed in foster care. Miracle of miracles, I was now being told my mother made a recovery and wanted to meet me. Surprise of surprises, I was told I had an older sister on the other side of town. I wasn't interested in other mothers. I certainly wasn't interested in older sisters. I was the oldest in my family. I was the big sister!

WE DIDN'T HAVE THE INCENTIVE TO GET TO KNOW EACH OTHER.

For the next ten years in foster care, my sister, Andi, and I didn't have the incentive to get to know each other and build a relationship. While my journey in the system was kept a secret, everyone in her circles knew about her "other family." I didn't want to give her the time of day. I didn't want anyone to look at me differently or feel sorry for me.

Andi lived on the south side of town. I lived on the north side. She had curly hair and I had straight hair. She wore jeans and I wore dresses. I thought those were good enough reasons not to get to know her as a friend, let alone a sister.

Then, the fateful day arrived. Andi was living the college life and I was finishing up my junior year in high school. She invited me to spend a weekend with her *on campus. While I was hesitant, I was just starting to realize that this person, my sister, wouldn't let up on me. She wanted to get to know me. Perhaps, I thought, it was time to get to know her.*

As we approached her apartment, Andi appeared curbside with a hand outstretched and a soft, sure smile. I slowly ventured out of the car and with a nervous smile back, I gave her a hug. The first thing she said to me with hopeful eyes was, "Can I introduce you as my little sister?"

All of a sudden I was embarrassed for all the years I never gave her

> *I* WAS EMBARRASSED FOR ALL THE YEARS I NEVER GAVE HER THE TIME OF DAY.

the time of day. Before me was a person who already told the world I was her sister and she was proud. She wanted to share her little sister. I wanted her to be my big sister. Through tears I answered, "I would really like that." She told everyone about her little sister. Little did I know the champion she was about to become as we grew together as adult sisters and friends.

She treated me as a celebrity, boasting about my activities in high school to all her friends. She came to visit me at college and cheered my sorority leadership, joking that while I was an SDT (Sigma Delta Tau) she was a GDI (Gosh Darn Independent).

She met me on the road during my corporate life—sitting in audiences, being the first to applaud my words of wisdom. She was all too excited to become Auntie Andi and develop meaningful relationships with my children. She was excited about my quest to be an entrepreneur and celebrated the opening of my company.

Above all, it was my proclamation of a new idea that mutually honored our sibling connection, which oozed with championship.

When I was forty years old and Andi was forty-two, I asked her what she thought about starting a camp for brothers and sisters in foster care. I wanted to give back the gift of quality time together and the memories that go with them. Andi and I didn't have either. Without hesitation, Andi said, "I never heard of it. But, if you say it is going to happen, it will."

> CAMP TO BELONG IS NOW A REALITY, DEDICATED TO REUNITING SIBLINGS.

Because of those words, I surged ahead. Camp To Belong is now a reality as a nonprofit organization dedicated to reuniting brothers and sisters placed in different foster homes for events of fun, emotional empowerment, and sibling connection. Andi and I stand before the children as sisters, role models, mentors, and champions.

Andi has championed me and our organization to creating lifetime impacts.

Because of this, we now share both our lost childhood dreams and our adult dreams with each other. As a special education teacher, and mother of three, she has been my model for accepting and celebrating differences. The champion role goes both ways. I tell everyone about my big sister Andi.

I still remember that outstretched hand and soft, sure smile. It was from my champion, my friend, my sister. I now exchange my outstretched hand and soft, sure smile with her today.

WONDER

Behold the child by nature's law,
pleased with a rattle, tickled with a straw.
—ALEXANDER POPE

Have you ever emptied a child's pockets? If you have, you'll have noticed that they are constantly filled with bits of string and paper, pebbles and rocks, leaves and flowers, and even birds' feathers—all the child's found treasures of the day. And, more often than not, if you are like most adults, you'll have emptied the pockets' contents into the trash, not placing the same value on the child's treasures. As we grow older, many of us lose the freshness of a child's view. We've seen the same thing so many times that we take what we see for granted. Some of us even stop seeing certain things permanently. Think about it. When was the last time you saw or heard about a Fortune 500 CEO staring in awe-inspired fascination at a caterpillar's cocoon or receiving an unparalleled thrill from playing "keep away" with a garden sprinkler jet—the jet whirling round and round, being dodged by the CEO, who is the only other participant in the game? Not often, right?

A sense of wonder is not usually at the top of the list when individuals are asked what is important. Very often, food, clothing, and shelter "hit" the top slots. But, without wonder and the opportunity to learn new things, children of all ages lose an important part of themselves.

Sky-high enthusiasm
by Krishna San Nicolas

My daughter Karis is a very daring and curious soul. She doesn't hesitate *to jump into anything. Because of this insistent sense of wonder and need for adventure, Karis' father and I are amazed (when we are not suffering anxiety attacks) by her every action.*

Karis and I recently visited my family in Texas. It was the fifth time Karis had flown, but it was the first time she was old enough to understand what was going on. From the moment I mentioned the flight, it was all she could talk about. Every day leading up to our trip she explained to her daycare pals that she was taking the plane, the car, the train, and the rocket to Texas—all of them!

At the airport, Karis was glued to the large windows looking out at the planes. "Mommy! The airplane is leaving us!" she yelled out in upset, and pointed at each plane moving away from the gates. Once on board our plane, and in our seats, a happier Karis assumed the role of stewardess and greeted all nearby passengers with her very welcoming, "Hi! What's your name? You're going on a plane too? I'm going to Texas to see my grandma."

Then came the gadgets. Ever wonder how many times a child can take down

KARIS ASSUMED THE ROLE OF STEWARDESS AND GREETED ALL NEARBY PASSENGERS.

and put up a tray? Looking up, Karis soon discovered the reading light and air buttons. "I need air, Mommy" or "I want light" were her never-ending requests. The window shade was in constant motion too. First up, then down—open and close. She even asked me if she could open and close other people's window shades! Karis was in full exploration mode and had me asking myself, "Are we landing anytime soon? Please!"

Surprisingly enough, after getting off the plane, an older woman came up to us and commented that Karis had behaved very well, when all along I had worried that

my daughter was driving everyone nuts!

As an adult, I've found that I sometimes lose that sense of wonder I see every day in Karis. What she found fun and exciting about an airplane ride, I typically found ordinary and routine. The gift of Karis to my life has given me the opportunity to see all of life's wonders for the first time again. It has also reminded me that asking "Why?" and "Are we there yet?" twenty million times a day isn't necessarily a bad thing.

CURIOSITY

*He who has a strong why
can bear almost any how.*
—FREDRICH NIETZSCHE

When Carol Curren shared the following story with me, I was reminded of a child in an amusement park who, overwhelmed by all the new sights and things to try, often, without intending to be bad, spins off in directions his parents can't always follow. What often seems like a badly behaving child is in reality a child overwhelmed and curious about everything around him. This quality of constant curiosity and wonder may propel him into trouble on more than one occasion, but it is the same quality that is more often than not contained in the make-up of geniuses such as Albert Einstein.

A PASSION FOR "WHY & HOW"

by Carol Curren

IT SEEMED AN ODD COINCIDENCE THAT BOTH THE TOILETS IN OUR HOUSE STARTED *backing up at the same time. However, it was not surprising that it happened in the evening, when plumbers charge overtime rates—these things always seem to happen in the evening.*

When the plumber arrived I told him that I was sure there was a blockage in one of the main pipes. What else could explain both toilets backing up at once? The plumber worked the rusted snake down into the pipes. It was only seconds before he hit the clog. He eased the snake back up to the surface revealing, of all things, a pencil! The plumber claimed that in his thirty years in the profession this was the first time he had ever dislodged a pencil from a toilet. It would not be his last.

While the plumber went to the downstairs bathroom, eagerly anticipating what he might discover in the second toilet, I took a detour through the playroom where my son, Cory, was deeply immersed in a computer video game. With significant coercion, Cory confessed to flushing the pencil down the upstairs toilet—and two more pencils down the first floor toilet. "Why?" is all I could mutter. "I don't know," Cory replied, "I just wanted to see how they went down." A two hundred dollar physics experiment…

Life with Cory has always been an adventure. He is an affectionate and good-hearted little boy who suffers from Attention Deficit Disorder. At age eighteen months, Cory ran away from home. We found him five blocks and a busy street away— a neighbor was carrying him door-to-door in search of his parents. By the time he turned three, he had broken three bones. By age four, he had been expelled from nursery school. But Cory is also very bright and blessed with a keen sense of curiosity. He wonders about so many things. His methods, however, seem to cause the problems. For instance, one day he swallowed the metal marbles to one of his games because he was curious about how food is digested. Then there was the time he wondered how the walls of his room, his furniture, his clothes, and his body would look painted in white Desitin ointment. And, of course, I don't think I'll ever forget the day Cory wanted to see how his goldfish would fare in a saltwater environment.

Although Cory finds himself in trouble fairly often, I truly believe that someday he will do great things with all this wonder and curiosity. Perhaps Da Vinci created his first masterpiece with Desitin. Maybe Pasteur used metal marbles in his first biology experiment. And I wouldn't be surprised if Sir Isaac Newton's parents had some hefty plumbing bills.

CHANGE

If we don't change, we don't grow.
If we don't grow, we aren't really living.
—GAIL SHEEHY

Change is the force that raises us up and the force that can push us down. It is a promotion and a demotion, a beginning and an end. However it is perceived, whether good or bad, the one constant quality of change is that it is always something new.

Change is, by nature, an opportunity to experience something new. How it is handled determines the direction our lives take. It is similar to deciding which way to go when faced with a fork in the road. One side may be a direct road to happiness, while the other a dead-end, requiring backtracking and loss of time. Whichever road is taken, the important thing to remember is that even if one of the roads you take offers more than you expected—good or bad—take it as a growing experience and move on, even if it does involve unpleasant backtracking out of a dead end. Charles Darwin once said, "It is not the strongest of the species that survive, nor the most intelligent, but the most responsive." This is actually one of the many lessons I learned from Angie Monaco.

When I first joined the ad sales staff at the Albany *Times Union*, Angelo Monaco (Angie to everyone) was the retail-advertising manager. Angie had a face that looked as if it was chiseled from a mountainside: deep lines, a permanent frown, a long oval face, all topping a reluctant shirt and necktie-framed neck.

Angie looked and acted like a "man's man." Although I never saw him smoke a cigarette, I never saw him without a long, black, ivory-tipped cigarette holder in his lips. It seemed more prop than habit and had the desired effect of causing one to look at his lips carefully when his low-pitched voice was whispering some instruction through and around that cigarette holder. Intimidation seemed his ally for any who had a direct reporting relationship to him.

At the time, my sales territory was the grocery stores. A major account was the A&P chain, which favored our *Times Union* only slightly as we had a Sunday newspaper and our competitor did not. A&P was opening their Albany Superstore, and all the national executives were to be in Albany for the Monday morning opening. Kick-off for the event was to be a two-page ad in our Sunday *Times Union*. I handled the account, processed the ad, and was frankly "pumped up" with pride at our coup of having the launch exclusively in our newspaper.

On Sunday morning I raced to get the paper and flipped through the pages looking for the colorful opening ads for the new Superstore. No ad. Sinking feeling. Disaster looming in my imagination, I drove to the newspaper plant and talked to the composing room foreman, who then chased down the original copy. The insertion date for the ad to run, in my clear handwriting, was for the following Sunday. I had scheduled the ad for the biggest event in A&P history for the wrong Sunday. I wandered out of the plant devastated, confused, and certain my career was over. Almost without thinking I drove to the home of Angie Monaco, who was just returning from church with his family, and who had not yet read through the Sunday paper. I burst out in a shriek that I had misscheduled the major opening ad.

I HAD SCHEDULED THE AD FOR THE BIGGEST EVENT IN A&P HISTORY FOR THE WRONG SUNDAY.

Angie leaned against the car, slowly took out his cigarette holder, managed that slim-lipped grin/smirk and said, "You cannot be telling me you left the ad out of the paper, can you?" "Yes," I answered. With that, he waved his arm, beckoning me to follow him into the house. Once inside, he picked up the telephone and asked for the home number and address of Jack Casey, the A&P regional manager. With address in hand, he stormed out of the house, barely giving me enough time to follow, and we drove to Jack Casey's home.

Angie rang the bell, and when Jack answered, told him what I had done. They both stared at me, and then Angie said, "We are here to start over and get four pages of opening announcements in the Monday morning paper—two pages in the first section, two pages in the second section, all without charge to A&P." Jack agreed with the remedy and the three of us set off to the newspaper to make the arrangements. On the drive down, Angie said to Jack Casey that we must keep in mind that the only reason A&P's opening day could be saved by running the double impact ads on Monday was because I had owned up, sought him out, and acted like a *partner*, rather than a simple employee.

I HAD OWNED UP, SOUGHT HIM OUT, AND ACTED LIKE A PARTNER, RATHER THAN A SIMPLE EMPLOYEE.

Jack agreed. Later that day a fruit basket arrived at my home with a message from Jack: "You Saved the Day, Partner. Thank You!"

On Monday I told Angie of the basket. He smiled full face—for the first time I could recall—and said that the life lesson for me was always to step up to the plate when a mistake had occurred. When one's purpose is clear, the largest mistakes can often be cleared up with what in the end feels like little effort. What seems like a mistake is, many times, an opportunity to prove that one can adapt quickly to change. It is also a reminder of how it feels to make a mistake and the importance of not cutting off the opportunity end of a mistake for oneself or for someone else.

GROWTH SPURT

by Matt Jablonski

ALTHOUGH I STARTED MY EDUCATION IN THE PUBLIC GRAMMAR SCHOOLS WHERE I *grew up, in Saddle Brook, New Jersey, when it came time to go to high school, my parents offered me the opportunity to go to a Catholic high school that my father passed daily on his way to work. Bergen Catholic High School had a great reputation for educational excellence, and I believe my parents knew that if I could make it through that system, I would be in a great position to get into a great college and a great career. Of course, they were right, but the thing that is most profound about the school is the fact that I was extremely surprised that it offered something special to me and the other stu-*

dents, something we had never had before—an opportunity to become young men.

One teacher in particular, Harry Murphy, would always address each and every student as a gentleman. Like any school, there are always bad apples. All the kids knew who they were, as did the teachers, but to Harry, they were all still gentlemen. It seemed like a joke at first when he would call them gentlemen, because they were everything but that. However, after only a few weeks, a strange thing happened. Those so-called gentlemen actually seemed to become real gentlemen. It almost appeared that if you called a dog "cat" long enough, it would start to meow.

Of course, I learned a lot of lessons outside of school too, but if I can offer only one, I would offer this: Sometimes you need to realize that the most valuable lessons you learn are presented in the most unusual circumstances. Harry Murphy taught me something very valuable—respect the potential everyone has to succeed. Through all the faults on the outside that everyone else may see in certain people, deep inside those people have the same basic traits you and I have. Instead of forcing others to adjust to your ways, give them the opportunity to recognize the value of change, and they will respect you for it. Harry never raised his voice to yell, but I believe his classes always had the best performance. I do not think a day goes by that I do not apply that lesson Harry gave me.

The Gift of Change

by Lishone Bowsky

Hello self. How's it going? It's been a long time since we really talked. A lot has changed in the last few years. I'm sorry that I've waited so long to talk to you but the truth be told, I couldn't deal with you a couple of years ago. You may not remember this, but you were hot tempered, feisty, argumentative, nonsociable, bossy, and impatient. You were angry at the world for being abused, humiliated, ignored, and abandoned, and it showed.

You fought a lot. You even tortured one girl so badly she ended up having to get a safety transfer out of school. You cursed people out. You were rude, disrespectful, and had a noncaring attitude. You didn't trust too many people, and those that you did trust had to work hard as hell to gain it, and God help them if they betrayed that trust. If they double-crossed you or talked bad about you, they had hell to pay.

I regret some of the things you did but you didn't know any better at the time. You were raising yourself and relied on instinct. For a long time people like your social workers, foster parents, and group home workers didn't want to be bothered with you. They figured it would be better for you to do your own thing and hurt somebody else, instead of taking the chance of getting involved and running the risk of getting themselves hurt. They had no patience or understanding for a child like you. You came from a rough background and had a lot of anger they could've done better in handling. It wasn't until you met people who saw something in you and invested their time in trying to change you, that you began to change.

Nowadays, you're nice to people, even if they make you mad, because you've grown too old to be flying off the handle. You've learned proper ways to deal with your anger, such as writing it down and discussing the situation in a calm manner. As far as people talking about you, you don't worry too much anymore because you've learned that people are going to talk and there isn't too much you can do about it. All you can do is live your life in a way that will make people say positive things.

Looking back, I wonder if there was anything I could've told you to keep you from doing what you did. Even though you didn't have a lot of people there for you growing up, you knew enough right from wrong to survive all you went through. Had I taken the time, the advice I would have given you would have been to listen more, to think before you act, to take a deep breath, to count to ten, and to walk away.

But while I can't change the past, I can change the future.

SECURITY

*In the long course of history, having people
who understand your thought is much
greater security than another submarine.*
—J. WILLIAM FULBRIGHT

Have you noticed the number of young children who seem comfortable wearing some of the most outrageous outfits in public? They feel completely at home wearing superhero costumes to the supermarket or even pink tutus with floral printed leggings to dinner at the neighbor's house. The thought that what they are wearing doesn't match, that there is no need to wear pants with a dress, or that a tie is meant to go around the neck and not the head, doesn't even faze them. They simply wear what makes them happy, not caring what other people think.

However, as they grow older, children do tend to take notice of the opinions of those around them. And, for those who are a little different from the rest of the crowd, this can be very daunting. Having a sense of security is as important for children as a compass is for sailors. If they choose to try something new and sail off course, they should feel confident in knowing that they will not become lost—that they are simply heading off in new directions and have the ability to return to traditional routes if they need to.

IF EVER THERE WAS A CHAMPION
by Arlene Cohen

IRA—A SHORT, BRIEF, AND RATHER SOFT NAME. HOWEVER, THE MAN I KNOW WHO *carries this name is not short or brief, and far from a softy. He is tall and rather hefty, and the shadow he casts when he enters a room makes him appear larger than life. Who is this lofty giant? He is one of the most generous, considerate, and loving people I have ever known. He has a passion to live life to its fullest. He cherishes every day and has no regrets. He believes in working hard and "smart," and communicates loyalty, honesty, determination, and perseverance. He has owned his own businesses and worked for others. He's experienced wonderful success stories and disappointments too. Through it all, he remains positive and optimistic.*

So just who is this remarkable guy who one month is feeding the homeless at a shelter, and the next month is providing transportation for a needy family? Who is this exceptional senior citizen who, in his seventies, can be seen scurrying around town locating hard to get "Beanie Babies" for his grandchildren, out golfing, fishing, or boating with those same wonderful grandchildren, and has done this for over twenty-five years? Who is this tireless man whose endless energy takes him to committee meetings at the community center and board meetings of volunteer organizations? Who is this wizard who works in his own business part-time, can play cards like a pro, and still gives a helping hand to anyone in need?

This extraordinary man has been a very significant part of my existence for almost fifty years. To say that he knows me, inside and out, is not an exaggeration. My father has been an advisor and a counselor. He has been a partner and a mentor. He has been a confidant and a friend, and he is my champion of champions.

Whether it was story problems in arithmetic when I was a young girl, or advanced math when I was a teenager, my father has always been there to assist. When it came time to attend college orientation, he was the one to make the trip with me. And, whether I was applying for a job or buying my first car, he was always there to help.

After being hired on the spot after my first interview almost twenty years ago, I knew that the values my father instilled showed clearly during that important inter-

view. He always said to set your mind to do something and go for it. Work hard and smart, be loyal, be honest, and be fair. Be good to other people and be yourself. In that interview, I was honest. I vowed to the interviewer that I would work very hard and not disappoint him. I told him I cared about people and therefore would be a natural in sales. And, most importantly, I was myself. I got the job. Today, I am still in media sales as a manager, and I know in my heart that I owe a great deal of my successful career to the lessons my father taught me. He planted the seeds and nurtured them. He still does that today. I have kept those same values at the top of my own "character list." I hope I have passed them on to my children—the next generation—and that they, in turn, will do the same with their children.

As I have always said, so much of who I am today I attribute to my father. By example, he helped shape my values and character. He was a definite influence in my approach to major life decisions. Whether it was college selection, deciding to marry, deciding to divorce, making career choices, or deciding to remarry, his basic credo of being true to one's self had a major impact on the judgments I made, and still does. We have a very special relationship, one that I do not take for granted. Not only am I very proud to be his daughter, I am honored.

Spiritual Oasis

HER VISION BUILT MY LIBRARY

by Robin Sidel

As a nationally-known educator and scholar, it seems only natural that Vartan Gregorian would be part of the prestigious panels that selected the Modern Library's "100 Best Novels" and "100 Best Nonfiction Books" of the 20th century. Over the years, Gregorian's love of books has been the root of his life's work, from his presidency of elite Brown University to his tireless effort in revitalizing the New York Public Library system in the 1980s.

But the woman who inspired his passion for books never knew how to read.

Voski Mirzoian was a proud peasant woman with piercing dark eyes and a difficult life in Tabriz, Iran. She was a widow who had buried her seven children, including Gregorian's twenty-six-year-old mother, and who also raised her seven-year-old grandson and his sister after their father went to fight in World War II.

"Her suffering, her generosity of spirit, her kindness and dignity, her love for my sister and me, sustained me. Her line was that I had a duty to live the lives of all the unspent lives (her children), to fulfill them, and that my mother would be proud of me if she was alive. It was very subtle and psychological," said Gregorian.

She was a striking figure, standing about 5'6", permanently dressed in mourning black with multiple layers of clothing (two skirts and one apron) and a purse tucked underneath. As a modest Christian, she always wore a scarf that covered her head and neck, and her eyes were like a radar screen. "They would go through you like an MRI," Gregorian remembered.

HER GENEROSITY OF SPIRIT, HER KINDNESS AND DIGNITY, SUSTAINED ME.

She was also the sole constant in the life of a young boy who had lost his mother and rarely saw his father. Although the family lived in their own house, her income was minimal.

"I'm sure she did domestic work without us knowing. I do not know what she did to keep us alive. But she was always there when I came home," Gregorian said.

And when he returned home from school each day, his grandmother would insist that he study for three hours. If he completed his homework before the mandated time, she would make him review it over and over again.

SHE NEVER TOLD HIM THAT SHE DIDN'T KNOW HOW TO READ.

She never told her grandson that she didn't know how to read, but always passed any letters and papers to him, saying "You read it for me." And Gregorian, who developed a love of reading at an early age, would sit down with her each day and read aloud from his books, often sad tales about orphan children. In return, she would tell him stories, recounting ancient parables that were often frightening and gory, but instilled a sense of right and wrong in the young boy.

His father remarried some years later and problems immediately developed. Gregorian was unwilling to accept a stepmother and his grandmother had a difficult time accepting the unfamiliar woman who had replaced her daughter's role in the family. The conflicts forced Voski to move out of the house and into an apartment next door.

When the young Vartan wasn't visiting his grandmother, he found solace in the neighborhood library, which was located on top of the residence of the local diocese. He read hundreds of books there and began cataloging the thousands of volumes.

But it was his grandmother who continued to be the source of his affection and protection. Convinced that adults should not hurt children, she marched into his school one day and slapped the principal because he had beaten her grandson for throwing a snowball that had hit him by accident.

> SHE WAS CONVINCED THAT ADULTS SHOULD NOT HURT CHILDREN.

As devoted as she was to young Vartan, it was Voski who knew the time had come to let go. At the age of fourteen, the young boy, unhappy with his home life and eager to discover the world, wanted to leave Tabriz to study in the more sophisticated Beirut, Lebanon. Vartan's father agreed to let him leave if he could secure the proper documentation, thinking that his son would not be permitted to get a passport. But he misjudged his son's determination, and after six months of working the government system, Vartan got a passport.

Shocked that his plan had backfired, his father refused to give permission to let Vartan go and said the final decision must come from the family matriarch, believing she would never let her beloved grandson leave Tabriz.

He was wrong.

"My grandmother said I had to go. She said, 'Get educated and you will become a man,'" Gregorian said.

He followed her instructions and embarked on a journey that would take him as a student to Beirut, and to America, where he would earn an undergraduate degree at Stanford University, and pursue his studies there until receiving a Ph.D in history and humanities in 1964. Along the way, he wrote letters to his grandmother regularly, which his sister read to her.

"Of all the things my grandmother did, she practiced what she preached. She never asked anything of anybody. She always believed a useful life was very important and that a useless life was an early death."

Her influence has remained with Gregorian, who in 1996 left Brown University after nine years at its helm to become president of the Carnegie Corporation, the world-renowned philanthropic organization created in 1911 by Andrew Carnegie. (Carnegie was so passionate about libraries that he spent $56 million of his fortune to establish libraries around the world, starting in the late 1800s.) Today, Carnegie Corporation awards some $60 million in grants annually to projects related to education, international peace and security, and international development and democracy.

OF ALL THE THINGS SHE DID, SHE PRACTICED WHAT SHE PREACHED.

Gregorian has received dozens of awards and honorary degrees, sits on the boards of innumerable charitable organizations, and has had schools named for him, all of which prompted President Clinton to honor him, noting "public education has been his greatest faith and greatest enthusiasm."

Indeed, it is Gregorian himself who invoked his grandmother's creed when the Carnegie Corporation awarded $15 million in grants to America's urban libraries in 1999.

"Our foundation is about children and their future—their future, which is our future. It is about adults and their aspirations, dreams, ambitions, and journeys of self-discovery through education."

CHAPTER FOUR

Outlets to Discover our Champions

OPPORTUNITY

We are continually faced by great opportunities brilliantly disguised as insoluble problems.
—LEE IOCOCCA

Imagine driving across a long stretch of highway bordered on both sides by just about every pure bliss-inducing activity imaginable. There is mountain climbing and sky-diving for the more adventurous, botanical gardens with acres of beauty and land-scaped trails to ease the mind, and beaches with tourist-brochure-blue oceans. Perhaps there is an amusement park or two, a zoo, or a fair along the way for children. Or, for the sports fans, perhaps the opportunity to participate in a game with their favorite athlete marks each passing mile.

Now imagine not being able to get off that stretch of highway. For some rea-son, there are no off-ramps and the only option is to continue driving by all the things you'd like to do, wishing that you had the opportunity to try at least one adventure. That is what it is like to have no outlets—not to have the opportunity to try new things, be it a sports game or a good education—and constantly to wish there was some way, or perhaps someone, that could help bridge the gap between where you are and where you want to be. On the tenth of May, in 2000, *USA Today* ran a story entitled "The all-Ellison academic team." It was about Brooke Ellison, a young Harvard graduate, and how her family, more specifically her mother, Jean Ellison, provided her the opportunity to stray from the road she'd been driving and explore the sights along the way. The article explained, "Brooke is paralyzed from the neck down from a spinal cord injury that's similar to Christopher Reeve's. It happened when she was hit by a car at age eleven. She depends on a ventilator to breathe and gets around in a motorized wheelchair that she operates with a device on the roof of her mouth." It went on to share how Jean took "complete physical care of Brooke while she [was] at Harvard. She has attended every class with her daughter, helped her organize her work, even turned the pages of her textbooks while she studied for her undergraduate degree in cognitive neuroscience, a

SHE ATTENDED EVERY CLASS WITH HER DAUGHTER AND HELPED HER ORGANIZE HER WORK.

combination of biology and psychology." As the article reported, their efforts paid off: "Brooke just received a summa cum laude, the highest grade, for her ninety-page thesis, which she spent a year and a half working on with a voice-activated computer. The subject: the element of hope and resiliency in people who have been through major life difficulties. Brooke was one of three students chosen to give a speech on Senior Day."

What Brooke Ellison's mother, with the support of her other daughter, son, and husband, did was to ensure that Brooke had the opportunity to explore the sights on the road of her life. Instead of allowing Brooke to experience a life of limitations, they found a way to bridge the gap between where Brooke was and the places she wanted to visit. The following stories by Tess Marshall and her daughter Kristy Marshall also share the special impact one can make by introducing opportunity into the lives of others. They are both examples of how personal champions can encourage you to become a champion yourself.

A BRIDGE TO OPPORTUNITY

by Tess Marshall

MY NINE SIBLINGS AND I GREW UP WORKING FROM SUN UP UNTIL SUNDOWN ALONG-
side the migrant workers on our family's eighty-eight-acre farm. March through

October, we planted, weeded, irrigated, and harvested fruits, and vegetables. When we were not in the fields, we were at the farmers' market selling the fruits and vegetables we harvested.

Due to their own hardships, my parents did not finish grade school. Although our education was important to my parents, homework was not allowed until the work was finished. Even when there was time, it was rare that we had the energy left to study and obtain good grades. When we became teenagers, my father's idea of a date was having our boyfriends work with us. My boyfriend Roger worked with me for two years.

> **DUE TO THEIR OWN HARDSHIPS, MY PARENTS DID NOT FINISH HIGH SCHOOL.**

When I was a senior in high school, I discovered I was pregnant. I graduated two months before our baby was due. When Roger slid that thirty-five-dollar wedding ring on my finger, he had one dollar in his back pocket. Our plan was LOVE! Like the popular Beatles's song that blared from the radio in our '65 Chevy, "That's the only thing that we've got plenty of."

Our daughter Roshelle was born that August. Two years later she had a sister we named Nicole. I was twenty-one when I found out I was pregnant for the third time. Six weeks before my due date I began having strong labor pains and unexpectedly gave *birth to twin girls! Within a matter of hours, I realized that by the time I was thirty years old I could have ten children just like my mother! I decided then and there that would never happen to me.*

For the first four years of the twins' lives I looked like the Peanuts *character Pig Pen, except instead of a cloud of dust I had a cloud of chaos. Everywhere I went two little girls, two babies, and two diaper bags followed. I lost ten pounds and had dark circles under my eyes. When the girls cried, I cried with them. When they fought, I fought with them. I was tired of diapers, dishes, and SpaghettiO's. I was bored with morning garage sales, afternoon soap operas, and stories of Snow White and the Seven Dwarfs. I was depressed and had suicidal thoughts.*

THANKFULLY, ROGER HELPED WITH THE HOUSEHOLD DUTIES AND THE GIRLS.

Thankfully, Roger was very helpful and supportive. Besides working two jobs, he pitched in with the household duties and the girls, which gave me the opportunity to become very involved with church. I made friends with a group of young women and we played softball together on the church team. The pastor, Father Don Downer, was our coach. He was young, athletic, and fun. He was also intellectual, something I found my mind craving. After the games, my friends Rose, Jan, Chris, and I would literally sit at his feet for hours while he talked

about God and the meaning of life.

We began doing prison ministry together and Roger and the girls would join us volunteering at the soup kitchen. What our family found at St. Michaels Catholic Church was a place to belong. Father Don suggested one day that I attend Grand Valley State College when the twins began kindergarten. I told him I wasn't smart enough. I never earned good grades and was terrified. He offered to help me choose classes and register. My fear was so great that I asked him if he would take me to the campus and show me exactly where to go. He did. I took a couple of classes at a time for the next nine and a half years. My plan was to finish while the girls were in high school.

I majored in Spanish and did a three-month internship in Guadalajara, Mexico. My mom helped Roger with the girls while I was away. When I returned, the girls finished high school and I obtained my Master's Degree in Psychology at Western Michigan University.

As a therapist and professional speaker, my purpose now is to help others live up to their full potential. I am honored that I have the opportunity to be alive at this time and to give back some of the blessings that I have been gifted.

UNLEASHED POTENTIAL

by Kristy Marshall

I am one of about 32,000 people in the United States born with Poland's Syndrome. I have a deformed right hand and no upper right pectoral muscle. During the fifth to seventh week of my mother's pregnancy a circulatory defect occurred in an artery that was connected to the gene my hand and right pectoral needed to develop. My twin sister was not affected. I had a very loving family and did not know that being different was not accepted in our society until one traumatic sunny fall day in kindergarten. A six-year-old sandy-brown-haired boy approached me. He grabbed my hand and began to scoff at me. "Your hand looks like a foot. Where are your fingers?" I was humiliated and ashamed. I immediately pulled my hand away. Devastated, I ran to the merry-go-round to seek refuge amongst my twin sister and my friends. He chased and tripped me. As a result, my leg was broken and set in a cast, and I was forced to use crutches.

What I learned at age five was that I had to be tough, stick up for myself, and not allow anyone to push me around. I also learned not everyone was going to like and accept me. Without realizing it at that young age, I created a vision for my life. I began to live my life believing that I could do anything a person with two hands could do. My parents and my three sisters supported my vision without being asked.

I became more confident in sixth grade when I began playing sports. It gave me the opportunity to fit in on the court or in the field with the other kids. I had a burning desire to play in college and would dream about the WNBA before it even existed. Some coaches did not believe it was possible but my dad and Coach Gordon believed in my dream to play at the collegiate level. My dad would often shoot baskets with me at the gym at 6:00 A.M. before school and Coach Gordon would stay two or three hours after practice to help me. In soccer, I wanted to be the goalie and had to prove that I could catch a rapidly moving ball to do it. My dad, Coach Gordon, and even my teammates rooted for me.

My mother often quoted the children's book The Little Engine That Could, *"I can, I can, I think I can." The words I can't were not allowed to be spoken in our house. Whether it was tying my shoes, putting an earring in, or learning how to drive a standard, I had to do it myself. My parents would only guide me.*

I worked hard at being a good student and had teachers who went out of their way to support me. Math and English were challenging for me. I would arrive early before class began or during my lunch hour to get extra help. My guidance counselor encouraged me to apply to the University of Chicago. My dad liked the idea because it was a Division III school and that would give me a better chance to live my dream of playing sports in college. Four years later, I graduated with honors with a degree in

public policy, having played soccer and basketball for two years.

My family, teachers, and coaches are all loving, nurturing, supportive people who challenged and mentored me. They were put on my path by God and helped me get where I am today. Unfortunately, not all children are blessed with opportunities and supportive, nurturing, loving people. One day at the University of Chicago, I read Teach For America's mission statement: one day all children in this nation will have an equal chance in life. I reflected on my life and recognized how much I had been given. I decided that I wanted to have a part in that mission statement. I committed to dedicating my life to leveling the playing field for all children regardless of race, ethnicity, socio-economic status, physical appearance, or mental state. It was once said that "it takes a village to raise a child." Since my family, coaches, and other educators granted me the opportunity to pursue my goals, dreams, and aspirations, I have the civic responsibility to make a significant and immediate impact in the life of a child on two levels, as a role model and on their achievement. As a teacher in a classroom, I did just that. As a professional speaker/educator, my vocation in life is to unleash the potential of children and ensure they reach their full potential despite any hindrance they may face.

EDUCATION

A child miseducated is lost.

—JOHN F. KENNEDY

Reading, writing, and arithmetic. For as long as I can remember, these three "R's" have been considered the cornerstone of education—the three skills every child will be tested on far into their adult lives. However, there are three "R's" of a different sort, which do not receive as much attention, but which determine how far the lessons children learn travel with them into adulthood. They are sharing, caring, and learning.

In 1999, Jane Smith, a middle school teacher in Fayetteville, North Carolina, did something that few teachers have done for their students. She offered more than a lesson in education. She offered a lesson in giving. When one of her students told her that he was on dialysis and needed a kidney transplant, she offered one of hers. What this student's friends and relatives were unable to do, Ms. Smith was—she was a perfect match to be a donor.

Jane Smith's role as a teacher extended past the traditional three "R's" taught in schools nationwide. By caring enough to share so much of herself, she taught her students the greatest lesson of all—the power we each have within us to positively impact the lives of those around us.

A SHARED PASSION
by Ann Lovett Baird

DEAR MRS. ADAMCIK MADE ME KEEP A WRITING JOURNAL AS A SOPHOMORE IN HIGH *school. Little did I know that my English teacher's requirement of journal writing would affect me so much. Her high expectations guided my writing and provided a foundation for my life's vocation.*

God has blessed me richly by weaving the right people into my life. Mrs. Adamcik was the first and most powerful influence. In fact, I still remember her telling of her Czech heritage and where to buy the best-tasting collaches in the state of Texas. She had ash-blond hair that was always perfectly coiffed, distinctively shaped and expressive eyebrows, and bright bluish-green eyes. Though she was one of the most demanding teachers I had, I do not remember her as stern. I wanted to please her and make her proud.

When I did something well or demonstrated skill, she always celebrated the victory in learning. Mrs. Adamcik encouraged me to observe the world for writing inspiration. Observing even the most insignificant phenomenon now serves as a springboard for me. I believe that her encouragement to observe trained me to draw analogies to help readers understand a concept.

I first discovered my love of writing poetry and songs in those journaling days in high school. At the summer camp I went to, I wrote poems for the camp newspaper. One summer, I won an award from the camp newspaper editor for my poetry. Mrs. Adamcik's poetry studies and journaling had already begun to pay off.

Now a training professional, a position that requires writing and delivering training programs, I often find my inspiration by looking back on Mrs. Adamcik's class. When I review my high school journals, and see her guided words, feedback, and encouragement, I am grateful for her influence on me. Her shared passion inspired the course of my life.

DREAM CATCHERS

We have to improve life, not just for those who have the most skills and those who know how to manipulate the system, but also for and with those who often have so much to give but never get the opportunity.
—DOROTHY HEIGHT

Have you ever seen a dream catcher? They are traditionally Native American pieces of art that are round, with what looks like a spider's web woven in the circle. Although I've seen them as earrings and necklaces, and even adorning rear view mirrors, dream catchers are often found above the beds of their owners, to catch dreams. They sort the good from the bad, catching the bad in their web, not disturbing the good.

Fortunately, there are some champions who also carry the title of dream catchers. They are able to sort through all of the everyday issues and get down to the basic road map—the dream we would most like to follow.

Karen Babcock is one person who benefited from such champion dream catchers. In Karen's instance, her dreams could have slid into the night, had she not had the support and encouragement of several key individuals who kept her dreams safe and who also ensured that they were within reaching distance for her.

CHAMPIONS BUILD ON POSSIBILITIES
by Patricia J. Drake

A NEUROLOGIST GAVE DON AND KIYO BABCOCK THE BAD NEWS. "YOUR LITTLE GIRL *has a condition called Spinal Muscular Atrophy," he said. The prognosis was grim. Spinal Muscular Atrophy affects the body in a way similar to polio. Because there is such a loss of muscle fiber, most children with this affliction die young, as they lack the strength to fight respiratory illnesses. They do not have the muscles to cough or breathe well. "At best, Karen might live to be ten years old," the doctor, trying to be realistic yet gentle, told her parents. "Make her as comfortable as possible," he added. "To try to do more would be just a pipe dream."*

At that time, many medical professionals shared the doctor's belief—a child

with this condition should not go through the rigors of therapy because it would be use-less. However, this physician did not recognize Karen's strong spirit, nor did he realize the determination of Karen's champions to try to help her beat the odds. These champions would build on Karen's spirit and strengths—her possibilities.

The battle for Karen's survival began when Karen's champion parents challenged the neurologist's advice. "I said yes to this [advice] in the office," said Kiyo. At home it was a different story. Because Kiyo thought bed rest would make Karen's muscles weaker, she worked with Karen to get her moving. She lured Karen with candy. The treat was placed on the floor across the room from Karen. The little toddler dragged herself, rolled, and used whatever muscle strength she had to reach the

He did not realize the determination of Karen's champions.

sweet goal. Although Karen was successful at this game, her parents needed to find someone who would give her therapy. They needed help. Enter champion Dr. David Gimlett, the Babcock family physician, who cared enough to give Karen a fighting chance. Not only did he find a pediatric therapist for Karen, he would play a big part in shaping Karen's future.

Dr. Gimlett was there for Karen when she was sixteen, saving her life from pneumonia. And, as a school board member, he made it possible for Karen to attend regular classes rather than be put into the special education system. This was before the Disability Act and the concept of mainstreaming. Dr. Gimlett could not have known Karen would graduate in the top five of a class of 490 students, become a National Merit Scholarship winner, and a recipient of two full-ride scholarships. However, he recognized her potential and gave her the opportunity to blossom.

Karen was also fortunate to have as a champion Pediatric Therapist Linda Yates, now the director of Good Samaritan Hospital's Children's Therapy Unit, in Puyallup, Washington. At that time, the Good Samaritan program was in its beginning stages, and Yates had just started her career. However, Dr. Gimlett, who had his practice in Tacoma, had heard about the program in the nearby city. When the Babcocks asked where they could get help for Karen, Dr. Gimlett made a call. Yates remembers the conversation they had over thirty years ago.

HE COULD NOT HAVE KNOWN KAREN WOULD GRADUATE IN THE TOP FIVE.

"What would you do with a dystrophic child?" asked Dr. Gimlett. Yates admitted she had never worked with such a child, but said after an initial assessment, goals would be established, and a treatment program designed according to the child's needs.

"That's what I wanted to hear," said Dr. Gimlett. "I have this little one sitting on my lap right now and I will send this child and her parents over to see you."

"Although I had not treated a child just like Karen before, I didn't see any reason why my 'help each child maximize his/her potential' philosophy wouldn't apply," said Yates. When Yates met Karen, who was then three and one half years old, she realized what a challenge Karen would have. "Karen had a severe form of spinal muscle atrophy," said Yates. However, Yates expressed her optimism. "Things are not inevitable. Karen needed to get up and get moving." Yates designed a water therapy program for Karen. In the gravity-reduced environment, Karen was able to experience movement not possible for her on land. At the same time, she was breathing against the resistance of the water, which helped improve her respiratory function.

Splints were made for Karen's legs so she could stand and learn to balance herself. However, Karen wanted to go beyond just balancing herself. She wanted to walk. "Karen sets her sights high," said Yates. One day Karen achieved this goal. With great effort and with the help of the parallel bars, Karen walked for a few yards. "I am a walking pipe dream," she stated with pride. Champion Dad took the day off from work and treated his little girl to a victory lunch at the Seattle Space Needle.

Karen's determination and stubbornness revealed itself at a doctors' forum where she was featured as the "patient of the month." As a neurologist lectured about her condition, the little girl sat erect on an examining table before an audience of doctors. To emphasize his point that children with Spinal Muscular Atrophy had little muscle strength, he pushed Karen's head to her knees. While the specialist expounded on how she would not be able to return to the sitting position, behind his back Karen was proving him wrong. To the delight of the audience, she pulled herself up to the original position. The doctor, who had said it was "a pipe dream" to try to improve Karen's condition with exercise, had to admit therapy appeared to be working.

Many times physical therapy was not easy for Karen or her mother. "Sometimes I had to sit on my hands," said Kiyo. She wanted so badly to help her baby. While Karen's physical strength slowly improved, her mental growth soared. Karen attributes her academic success to her parents and to her teachers.

Physical therapy was not easy for Karen or her mother.

Both parents love to read and they shared that love with Karen. "I have been very lucky in education," said Karen. "I never had a teacher give me the impression I couldn't do something."

Today Karen lives life with the enthusiasm of a person riding a roller coaster with hands flung high in the air. Although Karen is unable to walk and uses a power *wheelchair to get around, that has not stopped her from exploring. She has traveled the United States, Australia, New Zealand, and her birthplace of Okinawa. For the past few years, Karen has operated a small consulting business, primarily performing marketing, writing, and editing for local software companies. She owns her own house, tends a garden, enjoys photography, and participates in a hand bell choir and several writing groups. She would like to become a fiction novelist. And, yes, Karen has a passion for roller coasters. She has ridden these and other wild rides at the Western Washington State Fair, Las Vegas, and Disneyland. Karen also volunteers at the Children's Therapy Unit, helping to raise money to build a new 42,500 square foot facility—quite an improvement from the one room where Linda Yates began her career, and where Karen first received therapy. In the last thirty years, this program has helped more than 20,000 children try to reach their maximum potential. Karen's is one of many success stories, and now she is giving back.*

"I want to help this group that helped me so much," said Karen in recognition of her champions at Good Samaritan. Now herself a champion, Karen invites others to join her.

The following is a poem Karen wrote when she was fourteen. The poem speaks of Karen's journey in living life to the fullest despite her disability.

POSSIBILITIES

I used to think

that my limitations

were more important

than my possibilities.

Unhappy because I was not

always accepted

because I was shy,

because I was different,

I blamed my troubles

on my weaknesses,

Never considering

my strengths,

wanting what I did

not have, but always

thought I needed.

꒜

But now I know that living

does not lie in limitations,

it lies in possibilities.

If I can feel love,

and sorrow,

and joy,

and compassion,

and if I allow myself

to be myself,

then I've always had

all I need.

꒜

Anything else is a gift.

On my own time

by Karen Babcock

My champions did not make me the person I am today—they made it possible *for me to become who I am. The skills they taught me, the self-confidence they gave me, the self-acceptance they nurtured in me—these are gifts that I will treasure and use throughout my life.*

It is tempting, I think, to try to overlook a child's weaknesses or problems. We want to tell our children, "You're just the same as everyone else" or "You can do anything you want," because we want them to feel included, we want them to feel confident. But I wasn't just like all the other kids—I had a disability that put me in a wheelchair. And there are some things I'll never be able to do. My champions never tried to ignore my disability or pretend it wouldn't affect my life. But they didn't focus on it either. They accepted it as part of who I am. And in doing so, they helped me accept who I am.

Unlike fictional characters such as Ebenezer Scrooge and George Bailey, most of us never get to find out what our lives would have been like had circumstances been different. But I had an opportunity a few years ago to get a glimpse of what might have been, when I visited my birthplace of Okinawa. While vacationing there, I was asked to speak to two groups of disabled youths, and their parents, teachers, and healthcare

providers. One was at a residential hospital, the other was at a school that only served disabled children. In both cases a fair number of the students had the same disability I do—SMA. All were younger than I, and therefore should have benefited from the advances in health care and in understanding what SMA is and how it can best be managed. Instead, I saw children who were far more handicapped by their disability than I, who were isolated from their able-bodied peers, whose only expectations were to transfer from a children's ward to an adult one.

They were amazed to hear about my accomplishments and my lifestyle, and I believe my example caused the students, and the people who should be their champions, to rethink their assumptions about what it means to have a disabling condition. But I, too, was amazed, and grateful. Were it not for my champions—their willingness to defy convention, to push for what was best for me, to trust me, to teach me—it could have been I in the audience, instead of behind the microphone.

So, no, my champions did not make me what I am today, but without them, I know without a doubt I couldn't have become who I am, nor grow into who I will be. For that, to my champions, and to anyone who acts as a champion for a child, I say "Bravo!"

MIRACLES

I skate where the puck is going to be, not where it has been.
—WAYNE GRETZKY

It was uniform delivery day. Eager eyes danced with youthful anticipation as each boy received his brand new maroon blazer, with hand-sewn emblem of the Boy's Choir of Immaculate Conception Church. Bake sales, cookie events, and walk-a-thon sponsors had each contributed to the several-month effort to fund the purchase of the first-ever uniforms for the first-ever boy's choir at the church.

Now well-rehearsed, well-dressed, and well-prepared, the boys found themselves invited to perform at various venues, including a rare appearance to audition for the famous Princeton Boy's Choir. Although each boy was provided the unusual opportunity to sing for the world-renowned choirmaster, one boy in particular, Corey Kotkin, was declared as gifted and invited to audition for the full choir committee.

As the only son of a single mom, Corey decided against the interview since he did not want to be separated from his mother. However, his sights had been sparked to a higher aspiration and he did apply to the prestigious Manhattan School of Music weekend program. Corey so impressed the school that he was accepted and offered partial scholarship. However, because he lacked the funds to pay the remaining tuition, he resigned himself to not attending the school.

When his mother casually mentioned the situation to Corey's original church music director, and founder of the boy's choir, the director determined that Corey deserved a champion. The tuition was made available as a supplemental scholarship and Corey became a full-time student at the Manhattan Music program.

This fourteen-year-old boy needed a miracle. He needed someone who could help nudge the door open for him. My wife, Patricia Brady Danzig, who is also the choir director who helped open the door for Corey's supplemental scholarship, considers Corey's rich voice a gift to all who hear him—an absolute miracle! The following story, which first appeared in the Albany *Times Union* on September 29, 1999, is a similar story of talent recognized through champions.

THIS FOURTEEN-YEAR-OLD BOY NEEDED SOMEONE WHO COULD HELP NUDGE THE DOOR OPEN FOR HIM.

SOUNDS OF SILENCE

by Tim Reynolds

Eric Lindheimer has been known to hit an opposing football player after the *referee's whistle has blown the play dead.*

Naturally, the opponent doesn't like it, but in those rare instances, Lindheimer just shrugs his shoulders, offers an apology, and heads back to the huddle.

No malice is intended. It's just that Lindheimer, a standout senior fullback and middle linebacker for Guilderland High, is deaf.

"I can't hear the whistle," Lindheimer said. "I just keep going. They say that was a late hit, and I just say I'm sorry."

Usually, so are his opponents. Lindheimer is a six-foot, 223-pound fireball who loves to play football. He bench-presses 305 pounds, squats about 475, and looks considerably more solid than the average seventeen-year-old.

"He is one of those rare kids who elevates everyone else around him," Guilderland coach Pete Schwan said. "He's the catalyst, the inspiration, the leader. He's special."

Inability to hear is his only physical limitation. Those close to Lindheimer say they are most impressed by his ability to speak clearly, a skill developed by hours of work

with speech pathologists.

"If I don't wear my hearing aid I can't hear at all," said Lindheimer, who is totally deaf in his left ear and has about twenty percent hearing in his right ear.

Lindheimer can distinguish certain sounds in his right ear with the use of the hearing aid, but he relies on sign language and lip-reading in everyday life. On the field, his eyes are his ears.

Lindheimer, who lives in the Lansingburgh school district in Rensselaer County, is at Guilderland because the school has a program for hearing-impaired students who come from as far away as Poughkeepsie. Lindheimer takes all of his classes with mainstream students, although he does get in-class assistance from an interpreter.

"He's not handicapped," said Karen Messercola, an interpreter who has worked with Lindheimer since he was in elementary school and signs in plays to him from the Guilderland sideline during games. "He's only deaf."

> "HE'S NOT HANDICAPPED,"
> SAID HIS INTERPRETER.
> "HE'S ONLY DEAF."

THOUGHT GOD WAS GOING TO TAKE HIM

WHEN FRED AND DONNA LINDHEIMER SAW THE YOUNGEST OF THEIR THREE CHILDREN *come into the world Dec. 23, 1981, they couldn't have been more pleased. A Christmas miracle, they called him—eight pounds, thirteen ounces of healthy baby boy.*

The next seven months were blissful. Donna Lindheimer was a stay-at-home mom, nursing and doting on her son. One late summer day, she noticed something was wrong, but not even a nervous mother could detect the gravity of the situation.

"The day I brought Eric to the doctors I sent Fred to work, thinking it was all right," Mrs. Lindheimer said. "But when the doctors sent me to have a spinal tap done on Eric, I thought God was going to take him."

Spinal meningitis—a potentially fatal disease—was the diagnosis. For thirteen days, Eric remained in the hospital. For the first few days, no one could say if he would live or die.

"I did a lot of crying, but I knew he was going to make it," Mrs. Lindheimer said. "That's what I lived on—faith and love and hope."

The Lindheimers celebrated when they brought Eric home, laughing and eating and drinking with friends while the guest of honor watched from his high chair. At some point during the celebration, Mrs. Lindheimer noticed that her son wasn't

making a sound—no cooing, not even the constant stream of "Da-Da" that used to pour forth.

The Lindheimers rattled Eric's toys next to his ears.

No reaction.

They banged pots and pans on the floor behind the high chair.

Still no reaction.

The life-saving medicine adminis-tered by the hospital had one profound side

THE LIFE-SAVING MEDICINE ADMINISTERED HAD ROBBED HIM OF HIS HEARING.

effect—it robbed him of his hearing. That realization changed life in the Lindheimer household forever.

"Our toy was broken, and there was no one to take the baby to and get him fixed," Fred Lindheimer said.

The next few years were trying for Fred and Donna Lindheimer. They strug-gled with their faith, both in God and each other. The disappointment of Eric's fate turned to anger for his parents, who wondered why this would happen. The bitterness strained their marriage.

"I wrestled with it, and of the two of us, I was more negative," said Mr. Lindheimer, a client relations manager with the state Dormitory Authority. "If any-

thing, when that situation happened, the family can pull apart or it can get stronger. And we got through it. I know people who went through this, who had deaf kids way back when. Some of those marriages, they aren't marriages today."

When Eric was two, the family—his parents, older sister Stacey and older brother Will—took a learning vacation to Gallaudet College in Washington, D.C., a renowned school for the hearing-impaired. There they received counseling to help them cope. More importantly, they learned that Eric's deafness would be a handicap only if he or they allowed it to be.

Right down to giving the family nursery-rhyme books and teaching them how to read the books in sign language, the staff at Gallaudet gave the Lindheimers new reason for hope. For the first time, they believed they could help Eric live and learn like any other toddler.

WE MADE A VOW WE WOULD DO EVERYTHING WE COULD FOR THIS CHILD.

"We made a vow we were going to do everything we could for this child," Mrs. Lindheimer said.

They would take sign-language classes at places such as The College of Saint Rose and the University at Albany. Fred and Donna Lindheimer said they still are learning the nuances of the language.

Eric took preschool classes in a special communications session at Albany Medical Center. When he was five, he started kindergarten at Westmere Elementary, which was a forty-minute drive from the Lindheimers' home in Troy but had a special program for the hearing-impaired.

Eric spent first grade at a school closer to his home, but his parents insisted he return to Westmere for second grade, and he has been in the Guilderland district ever since.

IT WAS A VACCINATION THAT WAS NOT THERE FOR ERIC LINDHEIMER.

Eric described his childhood as normal. He played Pop Warner football and soon developed his love for the game, "especially the physical, the hitting," he said.

He tried other sports, such as soccer and basketball. "Too physical," Eric said. "Not basketball, me. I was too physical."

Eric has other interests, such as snowboarding, fishing, and woodworking. In fact, he just built a dresser for his sister's baby, who just received a meningitis vaccination.

It was a vaccination that was not there for Eric Lindheimer.

Making up for lost time

Football provided no significant barriers to Eric until last fall, and the roadblocks then had nothing to do with his hearing. A few days before the Guilderland season opener, Eric was hit from the side during a contact drill in practice. The hit was freakish, and the result was a torn ligament in his left knee, an injury that ended Eric's season before it started.

"It was crazy," Eric said. "I couldn't stand on the sideline and watch the team play. It was too hard for me. Broke my heart."

Eric had reconstructive surgery to repair his anterior cruciate ligament in October. Rehabilitation for such an injury can take nine to twelve months, a timetable that jeopardized Eric's senior season.

"With some other kids, there may have been a question mark, but not with Eric," said Schwan, his coach at Guilderland. "I knew he would be back."

Lindheimer was tireless in his workouts. He added more than thirty pounds of muscle over the winter, spring and summer during his sessions in the Guilderland weight room. He even ran uphill at his home while towing tires tied to a rope.

"He's a leader, and he's what all our student body and athletes should be all about," Guilderland athletic director Mike Salatel said.

Said Schwan: "He works as hard as any kid I've ever coached. He's come back from his knee injury with a vengeance. This is his passion, and I don't know, (returning from the injury) may have given him even more drive."

> THIS IS HIS PASSION, AND RETURNING MAY HAVE GIVEN HIM EVEN MORE DRIVE.

There are few players in the Suburban Council—or at any other Section II Class AA school, for that matter—who are true two-way players, meaning they are on the field for virtually every snap. Eric Lindheimer is the fullback on offense, the middle linebacker on defense. In last week's game against Niskayuna, he didn't miss a play—other than on special teams—until 3:20 remained.

And even though Lindheimer cannot hear audibles and snap counts, his games usually go without a hitch. He starts the play when he sees the snap.

"(Communicating on the field) is not hard at all," Lindheimer said. "My interpreter signs in everything the coach has said. And if I have something to say, I'll just come out and say it. It's not confusing."

Lindheimer then relays the defensive call to his teammates in the huddle.

Messercola said she doubts people on the other sideline can detect the sign-

language system, though Schwan said he sometimes wonders about that.

"We have our own system," Messercola said. "It would be very hard for any-one else to figure out. I doubt they can do it."

"If there's any confusion, he'll just look at me and I'll know something is wrong," said Pete Schwan Jr., the coach's son and Guilderland's starting quarterback. "We've been playing long enough together that I just know. I treat him just like I treat Pat Geiger, our other running back. There's a trust factor there that's built up."

More to come

COLLEGES ALREADY HAVE EXPRESSED INTEREST IN ERIC, AMONG THEM VILLANOVA, *Yale, and Navy. Bucknell is actively recruiting him, and that's where he said he would like to go. He said he has no aspirations of playing in the NFL and plans on becoming a civil engineer.*

Those around Lindheimer marvel at how organized he is. He carries a plan-ner in which each day is outlined down to the minute. Even his parents can't believe how regimented Eric is. One day last May, Mr. Lindheimer asked Eric to help rake the grass. Eric complained, saying it wasn't in his plan.

This was no scheme to get out of manual labor; Eric had planned to study for the Regents exams that evening. But the lawn got raked, and Eric's scores on the Regents didn't suffer—he got a perfect hundred on Sequential Math Course III (a combination of trigonometry and calculus), a ninety-four in chemistry, and an eighty-six on the new six-hour state English examination.

Lindheimer has been equally excellent in the classroom. He is a National Honor Society member who never has had less than a ninety-two average for a quarter. He also ranks in the top ten percent of his 460-person senior class at Guilderland.

O N THE FOOTBALL FIELD, HE HAS HELPED GUILDERLAND TURN THINGS AROUND.

On the football field, he has helped Guilderland turn things around this season. Opposing coaches can't help but notice his presence.

"We just decided to run away from him," Niskayuna coach John Furey said. "He's awesome. Tougher than hell. He's a great football player."

The Dutchmen were 2-7 in 1998; this year, they are 3-1, with Lindheimer rushing for 195 yards and a touchdown on offense and recording thirty-one tackles on defense.

"This kid does not understand the word 'failure,'" said Salatel, the

Guilderland athletic director. "He's got tremendous drive. He's got unlimited potential."

It's easy to believe that Salatel is right, that Eric will accomplish much more.

He has come a long way from the time when his parents feared their son would never enjoy a "normal" life, that he wouldn't be able to learn and have fun like other children.

The Lindheimers count their blessings each day, praying together and attending services at a Baptist church in Halfmoon, where many members of the congregation are able to sign to Eric. The twist of fate that nearly pulled the Lindheimers apart years ago has brought them closer together.

"If someone told us he was going to be where he is today back then, I would have not believed it. Absolutely not," said Mrs. Lindheimer, who now works part-time as a nurse at St. Mary's Hospital in Troy. "As God is my witness, we believe it's miraculous."

Eric, however, says it's hardly a miracle.

"Being deaf doesn't bother me at all," he said. "Nothing's holding me back. I don't consider it a handicap. I wouldn't consider it as anything other than normal."

BE A CHAMPION!

The more you garden, the more you grow.

**—THE BOOK OF OUTDOOR GARDENING,
BY SMITH AND HARKIN**

As I mentioned in the Introduction, I am a product of the foster care system. However, it was an invitation to be the keynote speaker at an International Foster Care Professionals' annual convention that initiated my education on the critical issues of foster care today. And it was the intense focus on understanding these issues that led me to Conna Craig.

Conna was one of more than one hundred children taken in by Joe and Muriel Craig, a couple in Northern California. The Craigs happily adopted Conna when she was eight years old, giving her the singular joy of having a last name. Unclear about her actual birth date or ethnic roots, Conna's friends guess that she is Norwegian,

Latina, Chinese, or Hawaiian. Age and ethnicity are uncertainties in Conna's background.

What is certain is the richness of her intellect, which resulted in a Harvard education, and the spirited commitment she brings to her laser-focused efforts to reshape foster care and adoption in America.

Conna's honors thesis at Harvard dealt with the relationship between research and legislation on child abuse. In the course of her research, she traveled across the United States, meeting with children in foster care, group homes, and shelters. She explains that she "met many children who, temporarily or permanently separated from their families of origin, languished for months or even years in state care."

WHAT IS CERTAIN IS THE SPIRITED COMMITMENT SHE BRINGS TO HER EFFORTS TO RESHAPE FOSTER CARE.

From her personal experience as a child within the labyrinthine foster care system, coupled with her commitment to creating policy blueprints that would tangibly improve the foster care system, Conna co-founded an organization to focus with facts and intelligence on reshaping foster care and adoption.

Conna brought to this challenge her leadership power of innovation, creating the Institute for Children, Inc. After identifying the key factors that stood in the way of foster children securing permanent, loving homes, the Institute created strategies to restructure America's system of public agency child welfare. A key strategy of the Institute for Children is to help restructure the existing child welfare funding mechanisms in order to create incentives to get children out of long-term care and into permanent, loving homes.

Conna succeeded in demonstrating the power of innovation in 1993 to then-Governor William Weld of Massachusetts. Governor Weld responded eagerly to her proposed action plan, "What a Governor Can Do to Make Foster Care and Adoption Work." Following the implementation of that plan, the number of foster child adoptions in Massachusetts increased from 599 to 1,068 in just two years, and has continued to rise. Of course, many factors led to the increase, and the Institute for Children was a key player in the change.

Conna has taken the Massachusetts success to other governors, initiating and helping to create change in their state foster care systems. She points to the fact that nationwide, there are more than 53,000 foster children who are free to be adopted, yet languish in the foster care system because of a bloated social service bureaucracy that fails to aggressively recruit adoptive families, or finalize adoptions in a timely manner.

Conna Craig has infused the power of innovation into the Institute for

Children. The very charter she wrote for the Institute sparkles from her drive to bring permanent innovation to the entire foster care system; the mission of the Institute is to reshape foster care and adoption so that every child will have the chance to grow up in a loving, permanent family. The mission is achieved by initiating policy reforms directed not to building bigger or more expensive programs, but to caring for our most valuable children.

S**HE WORKS TO ENSURE THAT COUNTLESS FOSTER CHILDREN WILL HAVE WHAT THEIR HEARTS YEARN FOR.**

Conna was herself one of those vulnerable children. Her awareness of the "client side" of the foster care and adoption equation strengthens her commitment to ensuring that countless future foster children will have what their hearts yearn for—a mother and a father, and a last name.

Being a champion isn't something that necessarily requires giving away a large chunk of one's time, or going out of one's way to try to do something special for someone. In most cases, if we are open to it, being a champion is something that simply comes naturally.

Peonies are popular plants in gardens around the world. One of their striking qualities is their flowers. The buds form like small tightly wound balls. Gardeners who have grown these plants over the years will tell you not to worry about the ants that are attracted to the "honeydew" given off by the growing bud. As they move around the bud, day after day, hour after hour, and minute after minute, the ants help loosen the tightly wound bud—they help open the bud up to the beauty that lies inside. By doing what comes naturally to them, they help initiate the opening of what is without a doubt one of nature's most beautiful flowers. By following her instinct and doing what came naturally to her, Conna Craig helped open opportunities up for others to experience the beauty in life. The following piece about Dr. Arlyn Moeller shares a similar story. Laughter came naturally to this doctor. He lit up the lives of those around him with his humor by championing happiness.

Natural vigor
by Lisa Moeller

My father recently died. He died in the same manner that he lived: full of vigor and zest—*on top of his game, playing racquetball.*

He was a family practice doctor, a leader in the community, a mentor, an athlete, a musician, and a practical joker.

Many people have sent me sympathy cards: friends of the family and friends

of mine. But, I've been moved by the number of letters I've received from people I don't know or have not thought of since childhood. They all include such phrases as: he was my hero, he was my mentor, he was the reason I became who I am today, and he taught me so much. The other common theme each letter included was that he had such a sense of humor—how he made life so much more fun through laughter.

Laughter was a big part of my childhood and upbringing. My dad frequently used humor to guide us through life's challenges. Along with the package came his practical jokes—every day was April Fool's Day.

I frequently tell bedtime stories to my children and many of their favorites are about Papa and his antics: How he would lie on his back on the floor of his office and do 'flips' with his young patients to make them less afraid of the doctor, and how he sang silly made-up songs at the top of his lungs while walking down the street with me (and how I always wished for a paper bag to put over my head so no one would notice me). Once he dressed my guinea pigs' cedar shavings bag up like a person—in my bathrobe with a wig stand on top, sitting at my desk chair just inside my bedroom. When I went to go to bed, I flicked on the lights and immediately flew out of the room. Out of the corner of my eye, I had seen someone sitting in my chair. I panicked and ran from the room screaming. And as I made my way down the hall, I heard Dad laughing in the family room.

He never tired of these games. He must have spent hours hiding in closets and outside our bedroom windows, scratching at the panes, with his glasses upside down and a flashlight under his chin just to scare the pants off of one of us. My brother and sister learned that the less reaction they gave, the quicker he would tire of his antics. With me, he got a rise every time—and he loved it! People who didn't know him have thought I was emotionally abused, but along with all that joking was a man who had a deep love for us.

As a father, he taught us independence and confidence, and how to stand up for our beliefs. He gave us opportunities that very few people get in life—making sure we knew that we could change the world if we wanted to. I know that I will continue to be inspired by him in my parenting, in my work, and in my relationships with others.

As I wrote these words, I struggled to compose an ending to sum up the image of the man who was my father, but the end did not come easily to me. That may say a lot—that his life was not lived like one that had an ending. Although he left in such an abrupt manner, without even a goodbye, he left me with a legacy of memories and laughter that I can always rely on when life becomes too overbearing. I love you, Dad.

HOPE FOR THE FUTURE

*If help and salvation are to come, they can only come
from the child, for the children are the makers of men.*
—MARIA MONTESSORI

While researching *Every Child Deserves a Champion*, I was particularly interested in reading about the theories of experts in the field of child development. I wanted to learn as much as possible about the essentials of child development that needed championing. Although such names as John Holt's and Dr. Spock's were at the top of my list, I ended up becoming more intrigued by the writings of those I knew little to nothing about, such as Polish doctor and writer Janusz Korczak.

Although educators in the United States have been experimenting with "courts of peers" to discipline students, Korczak was implementing this system in the orphanage he was the principal of pre-WWII. He, himself, had to go in front of "the court" on different occasions to be judged. Imagine that, a teacher being judged by his students.

What Korczak is remembered for, however, is more for his dedication to the orphan children in his care than necessarily for his educational policy. During World War II, in the infamous Warsaw Ghetto, Korczak turned down offers to save his own life, and instead stayed with 200 of his orphans as they marched onto a train that would eventually take all of them to the gas chambers of Treblinka. Although his life ended so tragically, his spirit has continued to inspire millions around the world to strive to uphold, most notably, the rights he determined that every child should have. Listed below are those rights:

THE RIGHTS OF THE CHILDREN

by Janusz Korczak, doctor and champion of children

(as translated in *A Voice for the Child*, Thorsons, ©April 1999, Sandra Joseph)

I CALL FOR A MAGNA CHARTA LIBERATIS CONCERNING THE RIGHTS OF THE CHILD. *Perhaps there are more, but I have found these to be the principal rights.*

The child has the right to receive love.

The child has the right to respect.

The child has the right to optimal conditions in which to grow and develop.

The child has the right to live in the present.

The child has the right to be himself or herself.

The child has the right to make mistakes.

The child has the right to fail.

The child has the right to be taken seriously.

The child has the right to be appreciated for what he is.

The child has the right to have secrets.

The child has the right to a lie, a deception, a theft.

The child has the right to respect for his possessions and budget.

The child has the right to education.

The child has the right to protest an injustice.

The child has the right to a Children's Court where he can judge and be judged by his peers.

The child has the right to be defended in the juvenile justice court system.

The child has the right to respect for his grief.

The child has the right to commune with God.

Spiritual Oasis

*I*t is my hope that the stories in *Every Child Deserves a Champion—Including the Child Within You!* will encourage a higher purpose within you to be a champion for others. With these words, I leave you with the final Spiritual Oasis, the song "You Are Worthwhile, You Are Full of Promise."

YOU ARE WORTHWHILE,
YOU ARE FULL OF PROMISE

By Bob Danzig, Al McCree, and Jana Stanfield

Chorus: You are worthwhile; you are full of promise.

Angels in disguise reveal your destiny.

You are worthwhile; you are full of promise.

You'll find angel threads woven through your life, your tapestry.

A lonely foster child moved from home to home;

forced at an early age to face life on his own.

A caring social worker kept his hope alive;

inspired him to be more than he could see with his own eyes.

Angels in disguise look just like you and me.

If you listen with your heart, you can hear them sing.

Chorus: You are worthwhile; you are full of promise.

Angels in disguise reveal your destiny.

You are worthwhile; you are full of promise.

You'll find angel threads woven through your life, your tapestry.

There's a child on the sidelines, who's never asked to play.

When kids are choosing sides, she waits and hopes and prays.

Gives thanks for those who love her, her family and her friends,

who look beyond what's different and see the miracle she is.

Angels in disguise look just like you and me.

If you listen with your heart, you can hear them sing.

Chorus: You are worthwhile; you are full of promise.

Angels in disguise reveal your destiny.

You are worthwhile; you are full of promise.

You'll find angel threads woven through your life, your tapestry.

When life is full of trouble and the world is hard to face,

angels all around light the way from fear to grace.

So be a willing vessel for those quiet whisperings

and the guiding loving spirit that comes on angel's wings.

You will find your angels, like shelters in the storm.

They'll give you inspiration, words to keep you warm.

So look for ways to help the people close to you.

When you share what you've been given, you can be an angel too.

Chorus: You are worthwhile; you are full of promise.

Angels in disguise reveal your destiny.

You are worthwhile; you are full of promise.

You'll find angel threads woven through your life, your tapestry.

About the Author

Bob Danzig learned first-hand the unique impact champions have on children (those of a young age and the child within all of us). Having grown up in the foster care system, Bob felt his first sense of self-worth when the foster care professional placing him in his fifth foster home told him, "You are worthwhile." These words became a tattoo on his spirit, and remained with him his entire life—from the first day he walked into the Albany *Times Union* as a young teenage office boy, to the day he became publisher of that same paper, and then ultimately the nationwide CEO of the Hearst Newspaper Group and vice president of the Hearst Corporation.

Today, Bob shares the impact of the words "You are worthwhile" and "You are full of promise" nationwide. A dynamic speaker, he shares his own life stories, inspiring changes in the lives of those who hear his timeless message of leadership and success. These inspirational messages encouraging personal growth and improvement have also made an impact on those who have read his other books, *The Leader Within You, Vitamins for the Spirit,* and *Angel Threads.*

As a teaching faculty member at the New School University in New York City, Bob teaches the Confidence Course to hundreds of adult students seeking tools to enhance their personal, professional, and business confidence. Having noticed that confident people are successful people, thus successful organizations are organizations built by successful people, Bob developed the Confidence Academy, a nationwide professional development seminar that is based on the six-week long Confidence Course. Bob also continues with the Hearst Corporation as "Dean" of the company's own internal executive development program, The Hearst Management Institute.

All of Bob's net author and speaker fees are donated to charity, supporting students who have grown up in the foster care system (his passion) and gifted young musicians (his bride's—of over 40 years—passion).